P9-EMN-168

Withdraw
England Library
USP

The College Student's Complete Guide to Self-Protection

By D'Arcy Rahming

Published by:

Modern Bu-jutsu, Inc.
P.O. Box 703-A
Westmont, IL 60559

PHILA. COLLEGE PHARMACY & SCIENCE
J.W. ENGLAND LIBRARY
4200 WOODLAND AVENUE
PHILADELPHIA, PA 19104-4491

 # 25125089

Warning

The material included in this book is for educational purposes and to promote continued self-defense training.

The self-defense methods presented are not guaranteed or represented by the author or Modern Bu-jutsu to work or to be safe at any time.

In some situations, application of the techniques may not be warranted or allowable under local, state, or federal laws. No representations are made by the author or Modern Bu-jutsu regarding the appropriateness or legality of their use.

Before trying any of the techniques, which could cause injury, you should consult a doctor. The author and Modern Bu-jutsu are not responsible if any such injury results.

The College Student's Complete Guide to Self-Protection

Copyright (c) 1991 D'Arcy J. Rahming

All Rights Reserved. No part of this publication may be reproduced, stored in a retrieval system, or transmitted, in any form or by any means, electronic, mechanical, photocopying, recording or otherwise, without the prior written permission of the author.
Library of Congress # : 91-66909
ISBN: 0-9627898-2-8

Acknowledgments:

Editor: Jennifer Harris Baarman
Summary Editor: Kristina Lawson
Cover Design: Boecher Studios
Illustrator: Joe Garafalo
Legal: Alfredo Bismonte, Dr. John Lewis, Lou Bruno

Dedication:

To my wife, Benita, thanks for your patience darling.

HV
7431
R147c

Contents

Introduction   Pg 6

Chapter 1   Mental Preparedness   Pg 9

    The Late Walk Home   Pg 9
    Analysis   Pg 10
    Color Code   Pg 10
    Threat Assessment and Observations   Pg 10
    Victim Assessment   Pg 13
    Environment   Pg 14
    Weapons of Opportunity   Pg 14
    Mental Preparation for a Physical Confrontation   Pg 15
    Visualization   Pg 17
    Self Protection Drills 1-4   Pg 18

Chapter 2   Street Smarts   Pg 21

    The Jogger   Pg 21
    Analysis   Pg 22
    Racial Harassment   Pg 23
    Keeping Late Hours   Pg 24
    If You Are Robbed   Pg 25
    Escort Services   Pg 25

Chapter 3   Safety at Home   Pg 27

    The Stranger in the Dorm   Pg 27
    Analysis   Pg 28
    Physical Security: Your Dormitory Room   Pg 30
    Physical Security: Your Dorm   Pg 31
    Protect Personal Items   Pg 32
    Speak Up   Pg 32
    Off-Campus Housing   Pg 33
    Credit Cards   Pg 36

Chapter 4   Date Rape   Pg 39

The Date Rapist   Pg 39
Analysis   Pg 40
What Is Rape?   Pg 40
Myths of Rape   Pg 41
Prevention   Pg 41
Rape and the Courts   Pg 43
Rape Awareness   Pg 43
How to Help a Friend Who Has Been Raped   Pg 44
Rape Quiz   Pg 45

Chapter 5   Transportation   Pg 49

Public Transportation   Pg 49
Analysis   Pg 50
Personal Transportation   Pg 54
Analysis   Pg 55

Chapter 6   Drugs and Alcohol   Pg 59

The Party   Pg 59
Analysis   Pg 60
Legal Consequences   Pg 60
Crime and Substance Abuse   Pg 63
How to Conduct Yourself in the Presence of Illicit Drugs   Pg 64

Chapter 7   Vacation   Pg 67

The Hitchhiker   Pg 67
Analysis   Pg 68
Hitchhiking   Pg 69
Traveling Suggestions   Pg 71
How to Handle Your Money   Pg 72
Vacation Residence   Pg 73
Home Security While Away   Pg 73

Chapter 8   Common Cons   Pg 77

The Bank Examiner   Pg 77
The Pigeon Drop   Pg 79
The Woman and the Child   Pg 81
The Shell Game   Pg 82

Chapter 9   Choosing a Self-Defense Course   Pg 87

How to Choose a Self-Defense Program   Pg 87
Evaluating an Instructor   Pg 87
Evaluating a Self-Defense Seminar   Pg 88
Evaluating a Martial Arts Program for Long-Term Training   Pg 89
Evaluating Traditional Martial Arts for Self-Defense   Pg 90

Chapter 10   The Law and Self-Defense   Pg 93

The Bar Fight   Pg 93
Analysis   Pg 94
Self-Defense and the Law   Pg 94
Miranda Rights   Pg 95
What Right Do I Have to Defend a Friend?   Pg 95
What Do I Do After an Attack?   Pg 96
If You Cannot Walk Away   Pg 96

Chapter 11   Student Defensive Tactics Short Course   Pg 97

History of this Course   Pg 97
How to Use this Course   Pg 97
Principles of the Student Defensive Tactics System   Pg 98
Lesson 1: Attacks   Pg 100
Lesson 2: Evasive Body Positions   Pg 112
Lesson 3: Strikes   Pg 126
Lesson 4: Takedowns and Chokes   Pg 138
Lesson 5: Weapons of Opportunity   Pg 150

Conclusion   Pg 155

About the Author   Pg 156

Index   Pg 157

Introduction

It was January 15, 1978. Winter semester at Florida State University in Tallahassee was just beginning. Many students returning from Christmas break were moving back into dorms and apartments.

On this day serial killer Ted Bundy entered the Chi Omega Sorority house. He went on a rampage, bludgeoning two women to death and seriously injuring two others. Bundy was caught and after admitting to more than 30 killings, he was executed in January 1989.

Eleven and a half years later, on August 27, 1990, a similar incident occurred. Fall semester was just beginning at the University of Florida in Gainesville and many students were moving their belongings into their dorm rooms and apartments. The nation would again be shocked by the news of a serial killer preying on university students.

This time five known victims, four females and one male who resided in off-campus housing, were attacked. Some of the female victims were sexually assaulted and mutilated. The killer is still at large.

These horrendous crimes highlight two important problems. First, college students are sometimes specifically selected by criminals and second, we lack long-term solutions to violent crime. College students face great risks because of their age group, environment, and most importantly, general carelessness. These risks are not only from violent crimes committed by strangers, but also from acquaintance crimes of student against student.

For many students, going to college may be the first time that they are away from home. They face new peer pressures, new responsibilities, and the task of handling their new freedom. Self-protection is usually a low priority for young people, so they can easily become victims of violent crime and are often susceptible to con games, fraud, and theft.

Many of the nation's most prestigious universities are surrounded by very rough neighborhoods. College students may have only seen these neighborhoods on television or read about them in the news. In many cities, if a student walks within two blocks of a major university, he may walk into an entirely different environment from his seemingly safe campus. Students who live off-campus and commuter students have additional safety concerns about housing and transportation.

Some steps have been taken to address the problem of violence against college students. For example, after the University of Florida murders, university officials increased campus security and offered to house off-campus students in university buildings. Students' reaction ranged from using escort services more frequently and staying in at night to purchasing handguns and Mace.

A new federal bill was recently passed requiring colleges to publish annual statistics in several categories of crime. These categories include murder, rape, robbery, aggravated assault, auto theft, alcohol violations, drug abuse violations, and weapons possession. A driving force behind this bill has been the Clery family. Their daughter, Jeanne, was brutally raped and murdered in her dormitory room. This tragedy might have been avoided if she had been better informed of previous crimes at the college. The bill is effective because it will raise the awareness of students, enable students and parents to make informed decisions, and force colleges to compete on the basis of security.

Interestingly, these statistics will not tell the whole story. A requirement that colleges include crimes committed against students who live off-campus was dropped because of the difficulty in obtaining data. The recent University of Florida crimes would not have appeared in the statistics.

The answer to violence against college students lies within the student. Any other steps can, at best, only be a part of the solution. Crime deterrence will not occur unless students are correctly trained to identify and resolve potentially life-threatening situations. This book will help the student take responsibility for his own self-protection by providing him with tools to prepare himself mentally and physically.

First, the student will learn to develop street smarts. Students will learn skills of analysis, observation, and how to make themselves less noticeable in a crowd. Students will also learn how to lessen their chances of being selected as a victim. The information included here was drawn from many sources, including psychology, criminology, and practical experience.

The case method is used to set up problems. A short anecdote is followed by a comprehensive analysis of the situation and a discussion of alternative actions. Exercises, question and answers, and self-protection drills are presented to reinforce the information given.

Second, the student will learn how to prepare physically for self-defense. It is my firm belief that in a self-protection situation the student cannot rely on anyone to help. Even to have more police present can never answer the problems of acquaintance crimes.

This book will also address common myths of self-defense and the student will learn how to evaluate an appropriate self-defense course and the legal ramifications of self-defense. An illustrated example of a short self-defense seminar is included. In this seminar students will be exposed to physical methods of dealing with potentially life-threatening scenarios. The techniques should only be practiced under the supervision of a licensed, Student Defensive Tactics instructor.

View this book as a first step. Continued training will be necessary to realize your full potential. My sincere hope is that this book will find good use in the college community.

Chapter 1

Mental Preparedness

The Late Walk Home

Bill walked slowly, head down, shoulders hunched. He had spent an afternoon and evening intensively studying for his philosophy final in the library. It was a dark night as Bill trudged back to the dorm room and the backpack felt like it weighed a ton. Bill was so preoccupied that he did not notice a group of four men until he was only a few feet away from them.

The men stopped their conversation as Bill came closer and one of the men blocked his path.

"Hey, look what we have here guys."

The others burst out in laughter.

"Come on, let me pass," Bill said nervously. He could smell alcohol on the man. Bill had never seen any of these men before and since the campus was small, he assumed that they were not students.

"Well, that is going to cost you," said the man. Bill was distraught. He did not have any money with him.

"Please," he begged, "I don't have any money."

"That's too bad," replied the man. "We're just going to have to take our payment in punches."

With horror Bill realized that the men were now circling him.

Analysis

Bill was so preoccupied that he did not notice the men until he was upon them. This situation could have been avoided if Bill had the proper mental awareness. To develop mental awareness we will borrow a concept from police officers called the color code.

Color Code

The colors white, yellow, orange, and red are used. Each color represents a state of mind and an escalation in level of threat and action. Bill was in the white state, which refers to the state in which someone is totally oblivious to his surroundings. The yellow state represents caution. If Bill's mind-set had been in the yellow state, he would have noticed the men and possibly avoided the incident entirely. The orange state represents a state of alert. When the man stopped Bill, Bill jumped immediately to the orange state. This state is one a patrolling police officer might use. Physical confrontation is possible at this point, but the intended victim has time to prepare and possibly react. The red state represents physical confrontation. An attack has already begun and you are now fighting for your life.

Our goal is to raise the student's awareness so he is constantly in the yellow state. Developing your self-defense instinct will help to defuse certain situations and the attack might be avoided. When in the yellow state, here are some tips for observing and assessing the strengths and weaknesses of a potentially dangerous individual from a distance.

Threat Assessment and Observations

Sex, race, and height. These are the easiest features to identify and the most difficult to disguise. Keep in mind that these are for later identification only; stereotyping any group can lead to error in estimating a threat. For example, female gang members often carry weapons because gangs know that potential victims often ignore the women as threats based on their sex.

The Color Code

The white state   The yellow state

Weight, build, and age. Does the individual look athletic or very strong? Does he look like he could easily outrun you? Assessment of these characteristics may be essential to your ability to control the situation.

Demeanor. How does the individual carry himself? Does he look confident and alert? Assessment of these attributes is critical because they give you an indication of the potential threat's level of comfort in this situation. How a person walks, his stride, and pace fit in this category. Watch to see if the individual is ill or has any deformities or noticeable injuries. Next, observe the individual's behavior. Does he look nervous, or is he fixated on one target? Do his eyes appear fidgety? These are all early warning signs of potential problems that should raise your awareness level. If you believe that an altercation is possible, always assume that an accomplice is near. Do not get tunnel vision and concentrate only on this individual. Look for communication between this individual and another, such as a nod or similar peculiarities in clothing discussed below.

Hands. Are they in his pockets or behind his back? Is he holding his hands awkwardly, suggesting a concealed weapon?

Speech quality and accent. If an individual's speech is slurred, he may be intoxicated or under the influence of drugs. A shaky voice may indicate his possible lack of confidence. Accent may place the origin of the individual.

Clothing. Assessing someone as a potential threat on the basis of clothing may be difficult in a college setting where thousands of individuals wear various forms of dress. Look for badges or something that denotes an affiliation. Look for inconsistencies in dress. For example, if you are in a convenience store on a hot day and a man in the store is wearing a coat, your state of awareness should immediately jump from yellow to orange. In such a situation, ask yourself if the individual is possibly concealing a weapon. Gang members often wear excessively baggy clothing to conceal weapons. Look for inconspicuous bulges in the clothing

Facial features, scars or tattoos, and hair color, style, and length. Most of these characteristics are for identification only. But tattoos can give hints to lifestyles or gang affiliations.

Smell. The smell of alcohol or drugs should immediately advance your state of awareness.

Right- or left-handed. Note which hand the individual uses to point to something. Which hand does he use to reach for his drink? If you are attacked, chances are that he will punch or push you with his dominant hand.

Victim Assessment

Victims are often carefully selected; a random attack is rare. The same characteristics that you use to judge a potential threat may be used to judge you. The following is a framework to show you how to determine where you stand now and how to make yourself a less likely victim.

Demeanor. When standing, hold your hands at your sides and relax your knees. Your weight and energy should be forward. Walk with purpose, as if you know where you are going. Keep your back straight, don't slouch. Your body should be erect but not rigid. Look around to show that you are alert. Do not over-exaggerate or swagger because in some neighborhoods you could be inviting trouble.

Eye communication. Do not stare at individuals you perceive as potential threats. Look at them with your peripheral vision. Do not make eye contact as they may interpret your gaze as a challenge or draw you to their attention. For example, a beggar will search a crowd and latch onto the target with whom he makes eye contact.

If you are accosted, make direct eye contact to show that you are aware of the individual and that you are prepared to meet his challenge. If more than one individual confronts you, maintain three- to six-second eye contact with each individual or with as many as possible. Look at them in a random pattern and as you focus on one, keep the others within your peripheral vision.

Gestures and facial expressions. Keep a calm countenance. Even if you are deep in thought, try not to look preoccupied. If you are accosted, use your facial gestures to dissuade the would-be perpetrator. For example, a friend of mine was once walking home late at night from the library. A man stepped out of the bushes in front of her. She looked at him indignantly and asked in a loud voice "Can I help you?" The man was taken aback. He muttered something and walked off. The strength of her character was apparent and she may have avoided a potentially dangerous situation.

Outer voice. Breathe from your diaphragm to project your voice. Many vocal problems are related to improper breathing habits. Volume, pitch, and pacing are all directly affected by your breathing pattern. Do not speak just from your throat as your voice may crack, which makes you appear weak in the eyes of your aggressor.

Inner voice. Talk to yourself. Dissuade the voice that says, "I can't believe that this is happening." Tell yourself that you are prepared for this situation. You will not be a victim. Boost your morale with inner talk. Your inner voice will help you project confidence.

Environment

If you suspect possible problems in an area, make sure that you know all potential escape routes. If you need to hide or duck for cover, look for objects that might protect you. Cover is defined as something that can provide a barrier between you and the adversary and that his weapon cannot penetrate. Look for potential weapons such as a lamp, a table, dirt, an ashtray, or something that can distract the individual so you can make your escape. Remember, if you really feel threatened, you should leave the area. You have no reason to let your ego override your instincts.

Weapons of Opportunity

A major problem with carrying a gun or Mace is that you never have them when you need them. Most people would not use weapons unless they felt really threatened, but normally it is too late by this time. People also tend to become over-reliant on a weapon. So rather than using defensive tactics they become more concerned with getting out their weapon. If the weapon is lost or blocked, a defender then becomes psychologically disadvantaged because he believes that he has lost his edge. Another problem with weapons is that an attacker can turn them against you.

A better option is to use weapons of opportunity (or natural weapons), which can be incorporated into any system of self-defense. Do not concentrate too much on the weapon, but use it in conjunction with your unarmed defenses and not instead of them. Any room contains instruments that would qualify as natural weapons. These include pens, telephone cords, a stapler, hair spray or a camera strap. Even normal articles of clothing, such as a belt or a tie, qualify as natural weapons.

Mental Preparation for a Physical Confrontation

I believe that you cannot escape the possibility of a physical confrontation. You will be better equipped to survive an attack if you prepare yourself mentally to face such a situation.

In many instances crime victims die not from fatal wounds, but from shock. On the other side of the coin, people have survived extreme adversity through sheer willpower.

In early 1991 in Illinois, a young woman was maliciously assaulted by an acquaintance, raped, strangled, and thrown into the trunk of his car and left for dead. When she regained consciousness she yelled for help. The attacker then opened the trunk and slashed her several times with a razor, leaving her for dead. She survived for eight days in the trunk of her car until she managed to free herself and escape.

To reduce the possibility of shock, here are some steps you can take. If you fear guns, you might find it worthwhile to go to a gun club and shoot a firearm a few times. Not that you are going to carry a firearm, but shooting practice will allow you to get used to the sound and feel of a gun. If you have no self-defense training, you may want to consider taking a self-defense course. Self-defense training can help you relax, gain control of a situation, and reduce shock. For example, if you face a

Weapons of Opportunity

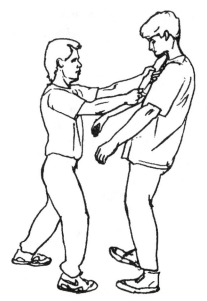

Defense with an umbrella

Defense with a telephone

Defense with a belt

Defense with a mug

training knife, you will be less shocked if an assailant threatens you
with a real knife.

Visualization

Visualization is very important preparation for self-defense. This is a
technique that is used not only in martial arts but also in other professional sports. For example, a baseball player might try to improve his
play by seeing himself hitting a home run. In self-defense you can use
your imagination to survive a real situation. You must be able to visualize the assault. Visualize surviving the assault. Visualize your goals.
Know your options because when an actual confrontation occurs, you
may only have one chance. Remember that you may face more than one
attacker. As you increase your skills of observation, you can begin to
visualize different situations in greater detail.

You must also be prepared to be injured. If you are facing an assailant
wielding a knife, expect to be cut. And if you are facing a club, expect to
be hit. You must have the mental toughness to realize that sometime
you may see your own blood. But it's far better to survive with a few
stitches than to have your life taken.

Self-Protection Drill 1   (Identifying Potential Victims)

Take a walk on your campus and observe the behavior and dress of several students. Do this again and don't stare too intently at any one particular student. This should be a quick scan. Consider the criteria used to evaluate potential victims and make a checklist to determine which people are likely victims and what they could do to avoid becoming victims. Pay close attention to the people who stand out and the people you hardly notice.

Self-Protection Drill 2   (Invisibility)

When you are in a classroom listening to a teacher's lecture, stare intently at the teacher. Give him reassuring nods. After a while, do not focus your attention on him. Instead, look away or pretend to be disinterested. In this way you can practice capturing somebody's attention and slipping away from somebody's attention.

Self-Protection Drill 3   (Visualization)

Read the crime section in the newspaper of a major city and imagine yourself in a situation similar to the victim of a particular crime. Could you have defended yourself or possibly avoided the incident? Remember the concept of the color code and try to apply it in actual situations.

Self-Protection Drill 4 (Breathing)

The goal of this drill is to help you control panic and bring your emotions under control by concentrating on your breathing. This drill will also help you with your voice control.

- Place your hands on your stomach.
- Breathe in deeply through your nose. Push your stomach and lower rib cage out as you breathe in.
- Exhale slowly through your mouth. Yell "Hah!" until you have pushed all of the air out of your lungs.
- Repeat first two steps, but exhale more sharply yelling, "No!"

Chapter 2

Street Smarts

The Jogger

Joan glanced at her watch and smiled. It was a beautiful morning for jogging near campus and she was doing her personal best time. As she jogged, music from her Walkman filled her ears. Joan always ran on the sidewalk, so she did not give much thought to traffic flow. She liked to run at this time because few people were out and the sidewalks were clear.

She was surprised when she heard the blaring horn of a car next to her. She looked over to see a dilapidated Chevrolet that was keeping pace with her. Two men were in the car and they were saying something to her, but she could not hear them.

Thinking that they were asking for directions, she took off her headphones and jogged over to the car.

"Hey chink, where are you going in such a hurry? Need a lift?" the man asked, taunting. The driver of the car began laughing. Joan was shocked because she thought she recognized the speaker from one of her psychology classes.

"That's not funny!" she said, continuing to jog. Joan's grandparents had come from Korea many years ago. She was always annoyed when people assumed that all Orientals were from mainland China.

Joan glanced over her shoulder nervously. The car continued to follow her. Joan wanted to shut out the taunts, so she turned up the volume on her Walkman. When she looked again to see if the car was still following her, she was shocked to see that one of its occupants had jumped out and was jogging behind her.

Analysis

Joan's lack of awareness was easily perceived and made her a potential victim. She was in the white state because she was wearing headphones. If you are going to wear headphones while running, do so on an indoor track or in the presence of many people. You should never wear them late at night. If Joan had realized the men were following her, she could have just crossed the street.

If someone stops you, even if just for directions, you should reply from a distance of at least two steps away. The men in the car could have knocked Joan down with the car door or pulled her into the car as soon as she got close enough.

Don't jog with headphones on outdoors.

Joan chose this time to jog because few people were out. In that case, she should always run with a friend. She also should have jogged facing traffic so she would not have been surprised by the car coming from behind. Once Joan realized that she had a problem she should have run away as fast as she could in the opposite direction (only if it did not bring her closer to the men). If they continued to follow her, she should have run to a more public place or started screaming for help. Any of these tactics would have made the aggressors realize she was aware of their presence, which in itself might have been a distraction.

Her less wise alternative was to have ignored the men. The confronter's intention may have been only verbal and "just to have a little fun" with Joan. She could have given him his "bragging rights" by letting him blow off steam and satisfy his ego. This strategy is risky because the loudmouth may be bolstering himself up to attack. Or worse, he may be trying to distract you so that his accomplices can encircle you. You can never take such a chance. Your best reaction is to run away.

Additionally, never, never carry your keys with your identification. If they are stolen you don't want someone to match a key with an address. Instead, for example, put your key in your shoe and your identification in your pocket. If you do lose your keys and your identification in the same place, go home and have the locks changed right away.

On a deserted street, stay in the middle of the sidewalk, not too close to a building where someone can reach out and grab you. But do not walk or jog too close to the curb where someone in a car can pull up to you and easily grab you. Also be careful of cars parked by the curb as a driver may be waiting to ambush you.

Familiarize yourself with alternative routes to your destination and vary your routes. Often victims are closely watched for some time before an assault. When entering a building or car, always do a 180-degree turn.

Recently in Illinois a young female student was found brutally murdered outside of her car in a parking lot. Her assailant had followed her and then waited between two parked cars.

Racial Harassment

Unfortunately, Joan was also the victim of racial harassment, which is not uncommon on college campuses. A constant debate rages in the media and in political circles about implementing policies to attract minority groups to colleges. This debate has sparked many racial incidents. Further problems occur when homogeneous groups try to further their own causes.

Campuses are still somewhat segregated. This is never an actual college policy as discrimination on the basis of race is not tolerated. But self-segregation often occurs. People divide themselves into groups that have some common characteristic, which too often is race.

Once this division occurs, problems eventually erupt. College is supposed to be a time of great learning, not only academics, but also cultural learning. Students should take the opportunity to learn more about their neighbors and break down the barriers.

One of the best ways to respond to racial taunts is to ignore the words and then report the incident. No college official will ignore your charge and an investigation may embarrass and lead to the prosecution of the perpetrators.

Keeping Late Hours

If you study late at night at the library, take fewer books with you as your load will be lighter if you need to run. Wear shoes that you can run in if necessary. If getting to or coming from the library presents a potential self-protection problem, consider studying in your dorm room or in a college lounge.

If you have been studying for long hours at the library, consciously escalate your state of awareness to the yellow state before you leave. This may entail taking a short break to clear your mind. Use this time to talk to friends, drink or eat something, or run cold water over your face.

Many campuses have implemented a whistle-stop program. If a student is harassed, he can blow the whistle and immediately campus police and other students will be notified. I recommend that if you carry a whistle, do not wear it around your neck as a determined aggressor may use the cord to choke you or pull you down.

Don't exercise in public places during very early or very late hours, or in isolated places by yourself. If you jog, vary your route and the time, always staying on lighted pathways. Stay alert for anybody who might be watching you.

If you are going to be studying late at night in the dorm, make sure you have food, beverages, and any supplies you need. Avoid late night trips to a convenience or 24-hour grocery store.

If you are attending college in a new city or town, ask your resident assistant or an upperclassman to tell you off-campus areas to avoid.

If You Are Robbed

If you are ever robbed on the street, give up your valuables. If you carry more than you can afford to lose, carry it in a place that isn't obvious, such as your sock or underwear. But leave a little to keep the robber happy. Only when you or someone you care about are physically threatened should you take defensive action. Try to remain calm so that your attacker doesn't mistake nervous movements for an attack and respond violently. Remember that the attacker may be very nervous, too.

If you are robbed, give up your valuables.

Escort Services

If students exercise their common sense and walk in groups whenever possible, many incidents can be avoided. Most colleges have an escort service. If your college does not have one, obtaining college funds and student support to set one up should be easy enough.

Here are some things to consider when organizing a campus escort service:

- Approach a group that already has members and organizational capabilities, for example the inter fraternity council or an ROTC group.

- Obtain university funds and pay volunteers. If the escort service is treated as a job, student volunteers will be more committed to it.

- Escorts should have identification provided by the campus department of public safety. This will enable the college to verify the eligibility of the escorts as well as facilitate good communications between public safety and the escort service.

- A training program for the escorts should be developed which could include things such as self-defense, first aid, and knowledge of the campus and surrounding areas.

- Escorts should travel in teams of at least two, and be easily identifiable from a distance. For example a bright orange vest or an ROTC uniform. This uniform will provide a deterrence, because a criminal will know that it represents authority.

- Hours should be set and publicized so that there is consistency for the student users.

- During operational hours the escort service should have a receptionist. Each escort team should have a walkie talkie to keep in contact with the base or the department of public safety.

Chapter 3

Safety at Home

The Stranger in the Dorm

Mary passed the stranger in her dorm hallway. She barely noticed him because she was excited about going to a concert that evening. She was surprised by the knock on her door a few minutes after she had entered the room. She was not expecting her boyfriend Ed for another half-hour.

"Just a minute," she said. She opened the door halfway. Although the dorm was coed, Mary was surprised to see the well-dressed stranger she had just passed.

"Hi," he said.

"Hi, can I help you?" she asked.

"I live on the south side of campus and I heard that you had a stereo for sale."

"No, I'm sorry, you must have the wrong room," said Mary, as she attempted to close the door.

"Wait a minute," said the stranger, as he stuck his foot in the door. "Is this room 4A?"

"Yes," said Mary, now slightly annoyed.

"I have a poster here that says that someone in this room has a stereo for sale."

"Let me see that," said Mary, her curiosity piqued. She opened the door to look at the piece of paper.

Quickly the stranger shoved his way in, and before Mary could yell, he drew a knife, and put his hand over her mouth.

Analysis

Even the most cautious students may relax their guard when they believe that they are in a safe environment such as on campus or in their dorm.

Because so many colleges have coed dorms, a stranger who does not look like a threat is not perceived as a threat. Using our color code schematic, Mary was in the white state. She did not recognize the threat and although the stranger admitted that he did not belong in the dorm, she did not question how he got there. Mary was not wary because of the appearance of her attacker. She assumed he belonged even though she knew everybody on her hall and had not seen him before. When the stranger blocked the door, this action was a very clear signal that she was in danger. She was easily distracted and even wanted to see the piece of paper that had her address on it. Another mistake Mary made was that she allowed the stranger to shove his way in and draw his weapon before she could react. She had probably never been in such a situation and as a result, the shock of seeing a weapon made her freeze and gave the assailant time to attack. Mary should never have opened the door. She should have looked through her peephole to identify the caller or she could have demanded that he slide the paper under the door, which would have exposed him as a phony. You should never admit someone into your home unless you know the person or he is with somebody that you know.

An expected caller, such as a maintenance person, should have proper identification. But even identification in this age of instant photography and the personal computer is easy to forge. So make sure that you check it closely. If you have any doubts about the caller's identification, you can check with campus housing or apartment management. But do not call a number supplied by the individual. Look up the number in a telephone directory or call an operator.

A stranger wearing a uniform is not necessarily legitimate. Even if the stranger has phoned ahead and made an appointment to see you at home, make sure that he is who he says he is. Common scams often involve phony building fire inspectors or door-to-door salesmen.

If you are expecting a maintenance person, always use a chain lock as well as a rubber doorstop while checking his identification. A chain lock alone is not enough protection and is easy to break if you have a flimsy door.

Many telephone systems are programmable, so save one number for 911. If you are attacked in your home, help may only be one button away. Calls to 911 are usually recorded and even if the assailant were to hang up the phone, some 911 systems automatically determine the origin of the call.

If your room or apartment is broken into while you are home, you may have time to call the police. Be sure that you know your exact address and the closest major crossroads. If you are frightened enough, you may forget your own telephone number, so make sure it is on the telephone.

Having an unlisted number is no guarantee against a stranger getting your number. Campus directories often print your campus address and full home address, in addition to associated telephone numbers. These directories provide a wealth of information about you without your permission.

Always verify a caller's identity before opening your door.

A stranger could possibly use this information to try to lure you from your room. Be careful of the personal information you keep in your purse or wallet. For example, a stolen driver's license yields your address and social security number. If you carry pictures, they could tell somebody about your family members and boyfriend or girlfriend. Someone could pretend to know them easily enough.

If you do receive a suspicious call and you have recently lost some identification, be wary. Call the person they claim to know to verify it. If the stranger asks to meet you and you cannot verify his identity, refuse. Another trap is to lure you from your room and then rob your room. If you lose your keys, make sure that the campus housing or apartment manager changes the locks on your doors.

Physical Security: Your Dormitory Room

Take a look at the doors in your dorm room. Do they fit their frames properly? Do they look as if they could be easily wedged open? Can you open the doors with a credit card? If this is the case, door guards should be installed so that the doors cannot be easily jimmied. If a door's hinges are exposed, the door can usually be completely removed from its frame. Although a thief would need time to accomplish this, he would have ample opportunity when students are away weeks at a time during Christmas and spring break.

If a door has a small glass panel, ask yourself how easily someone could break this glass and open the door from within. Or if a door is flimsy, how easily could someone cut a hole in the door and reach inside and unlock the door?

Secure sliding glass doors by putting a short board in one of the tracks so that if a burglar breaks a lock or cuts the glass on one side, the door cannot be easily opened from the outside.

What types of locks are used on your doors? A deadbolt is the best type. A chain lock is a mixed blessing. If a burglar is trying to get in, the chain lock may deter him when he realizes that someone is home. However, the chain lock does not provide real protection because it can easily be broken. Another disadvantage of having a chain lock is that if a burglar enters through a way other than the door, the chain lock may slow down your exit from the room.

Windows are another security consideration. Windows above ground level will require less protection than windows at ground level. At ground level, windows provide an easy entry and a thief can see your possessions. As an undergraduate, I had a first floor window and people often came up and looked through my window into my room. Some of my dormmates on the first floor were robbed during spring break and the thief entered through their windows. Since a thief may have a ladder, all windows always should be kept locked. The only exception is a window that is used for ventilation. For convenience, a window lock that can lock in increments is best. Always request second-floor or higher room assignments.

Physical Security: Your Dormitory

Next, examine your dormitory. Make sure that proper lighting is available inside and outside the building. Hallways and stairwells should be well-lighted.

Here are seven questions that you should ask yourself to determine if your dormitory is safe:

- Are the areas restricted not only by building exits, but also by floor?

- Does the dormitory have hall monitors?

- Does the dormitory have an active sign-up sheet for recording visitors to the dorm?

- Is dormitory policy clearly stated?

- Do dormitory laundry rooms, washrooms, and public lounges require keyed access?

- Are emergency telephones available in public areas?

- Are dormitory policies followed?

Many dormitories have a strict policy requiring visitors to sign in and out after certain hours. And some restrict access to areas of the building by installing locks on hallway doors. The problem is that this system is violated so often that many students will not challenge a stranger. Often students will hold open locked doors for a stranger, letting their courtesy overcome their common sense. Assert yourself in such a situation and challenge the individual. If he has a legitimate purpose in the building, he can follow the system by producing a key or having his friend let him in.

One method of closely monitoring buildings is to install exit alarms on all but one exit. Doors with exit alarms can be opened, but an alarm sounds automatically when the door is opened. Disciplinary action can be taken against students who exit through these doors in a non-emergency. The alarm could also be used if a student were attacked. When the student opens the door, campus police are quickly summoned.

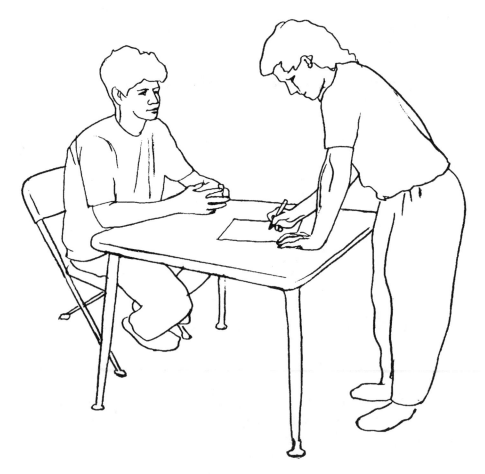

Choose a dormitory that signs visitors in and out.

Protect Personal Items

You should inventory all of your household items. Photograph them and record serial numbers, especially for big-ticket items like stereos and personal computers. Many students invest big bucks in electronic equipment. The equipment is purchased with hard-earned dollars, maybe earned by years of working summers or part-time at low wages. These items are irreplaceable in some circumstances. A lot of students also bring family heirlooms to college. If these items are stolen, they must be easily identifiable. You may want to insure individual high-priced items. Also they will be more easily recovered if they are registered. Electronic systems can be locked down by anchor pads to furniture. These anchor pads can be rented, with insurance. Unless the thief has the keys he would have to move the entire piece of furniture, which is unlikely in a dorm room.

Another way of protecting personal equipment is to have them engraved. Engraving makes them less desirable to a criminal because they would be too difficult to resell. People would be less willing to buy a item they know is stolen if they think that it could be traced.

Speak Up

Normally, informal rules exist within the college. If you feel that safety is lax, speak up. Others probably will agree with you. After assessing the security in your residence, initiate dorm meetings or seminars to discuss current security and how to improve security. Write letters to the campus newspaper or. many dorms also have their own newsletters. Take an active part in your residence hall. Voice complaints or suggestions to your resident assistant and neighbors. You must take a direct role in your safety. When personal safety is involved, this is not the time to be quiet.

Here are four ideas for students to implement on their campuses with the assistance of the college:

> • Emergency telephones: The telephones should dispatch
> police whenever they are lifted off the hook. Maps
> should be distributed to all students with the location of

the telephones. The telephones should be painted in a flourescent color so that they can be easily identified. They should also be carefully maintained.

- Dormitory-arranged talks with police officers concerning the level of crime in your area.

- Self-defense seminars and demonstrations to promote student awareness.

- Whistle-stop program: You will know a fellow student is in trouble if you hear the whistle blow.

- The student newspaper should publish crimes that occur at the university and the surrounding area, so students know which areas to avoid. Along with this information should occur safety tips that could lessen another students chances of becoming a victim of a similar incident.

Off-Campus Housing

Off-campus housing leaves students vulnerable to some different problems. A student may be more isolated in off-campus housing, unlike a dormitory or college residence, where he can usually count on the presence of other students.

Get a copy of your Tenant's Rights and review the codes. If it specifies window locks, peepholes, or wire mesh on the door windows, make sure that the safeguards have been installed.

Demand that you be notified if any maintenance person will be in your apartment. If you are at home, demand identification and verify it with apartment management.

Many colleges have legal aid offices that are student run and affiliated with attorneys. The purpose of these offices is to provide legal options to students. These options often concern landlord/tenant contracts, traffic ticket information, and consumer complaints.

If you live in an apartment, and can afford to, choose one that has a doorman. He will actually screen your visitors. Intercoms are the next best thing, but someone's voice can easily be disguised. Do not buzz anybody up without first talking to him by intercom. Often visitors ring each bell until someone lets them in the building. And frequently, residents blindly buzz in someone, particularly if they are expecting a friend. Verify the visitor's identity through the peephole in your door before letting him in.

A friend of mine routinely collected her morning paper early to prevent it from being stolen. In her apartment building, visitors had to be buzzed in the second door. When she opened this door to grab her paper, she would prop it open with her foot. One morning she noticed a stranger and thought that he was going to take her paper. She quickly grabbed it and turned her back to return to her apartment. She noticed that she did not hear the door shut behind her and turned to close it. She was immediately thrown to the ground by the stranger, who had followed her in. She screamed and fortunately for her, he panicked and left. Apartment security will only work if you think defensively.

All of the outside doors should be well-lighted. Check to see that your stairwell is well-lighted. If not, complain to building management. The outside of the building, as well as entrances to and from parking areas, should have adequate lighting.

If the doors of your apartment are flimsy and do not fit firmly, have the door reinforced or replaced. One way to protect a door that does not fit firmly from someone prying the door lock away from the hole into which the bolt slides, is to make sure your bolt is at least 1 inch long. If a door swings inward, you could also have an L-shaped metal strip placed along the inner frame of the doorway. This strip makes it more difficult for a criminal trying to pry open the door because he must gain leverage against metal as opposed to wood. Door guards or metal strips may be placed on a door that swings outward, thus protecting it from being pried open. Every front door should have a peephole and you should use it.

Window-unit air conditioners also provide a possible entry point for a would-be burglar, so these should be appropriately anchored to prevent their removal. If you live in a residence that has an attached garage, the door inside the garage should be as strong as your front door and similarly protected with deadbolts. If you were away, the cover of a garage would give a burglar considerable time to gain entry to your home.

The first thing that you should do when moving into your new apartment is to have the locks changed. This is the only way that you can control who has keys to your apartment. Protect the door with deadbolt locks that require keyed entry both inside and outside. Keep the key handy, however, in case you have to escape your house in an emergency. Internally, your bedroom door should also have a lock. Remember, a criminal will have more time to work in your residence if he doesn't have to worry about other students.

When you go out, you may think that you are clever to leave a spare key under the doormat or behind the flower pot. But these obvious locations will be the first place a criminal looks, particularly if he has watched you for a while. Roof doors should only be operable from the inside.

Fire escapes may provide easy entry to and exit from your domicile. They should be accessible to you and functional. A fire escape should provide a hasty retreat in any emergency.

On your mail slots, don't indicate your gender. Use initials and don't indicate which people live in which apartments. For example, if J. Davis, H. Sahara, and D. Bernstein lived on the first, second, and third floor, respectively, they should not have their names listed in that same order. Also, if you live alone, include a false name on your mailbox or list your name as Mr. and Mrs. Jones.

Your answering machine should not indicate who lives there or how many people live there. The message on some answering machines might be "Hi, Eileen is not here now, please leave your message at the sound of the tone." This message has informed the caller that only one person lives there and her name is Eileen. A less revealing message might be, "You have reached 222-2222. We are not here to take your call, please leave a message at the sound of the tone." This message indicates that more than one person lives there and gives no clue to their identity. Yet, the caller knows that he reached the right number.

Above all, try to get to know your neighbors. You should at least be able to identify them in the hallways. Find out if you have a neighborhood watch program. These programs might include block watches or citizens' crime patrols. Get involved. If you do, the payback is much greater than the time invested.

Credit Cards

For each credit card that you own, you should record the following information: your account number, the card name, its issuing organization, and a telephone number and address for reporting a lost or stolen card. You must have this information, because if you do not have credit card insurance and do not notify the issuing organization of theft, you will be liable for up to $50 of the illegal charges.

You can challenge any charges that are not yours. But you are responsible for the charges that you have made, so even if your card is stolen, be prepared to pay your bill on time. The author had the misfortune of having a credit card stolen. Although the loss of the card was reported in a timely manner, the new bill arrived with many charges pushing the card over its limit within three days. The charges were contested and the credit card company was responsive, but the author was never notified whether the thief was caught.

Professional credit card thieves often use a secondary market. They use the cards for a short time and then pass them on to an accomplice. This is quite easy, as many merchants don't bother to check additional identification or even verify the signature.

Follow these rules when using your credit cards and checks:

> •When you are signing a check, you need not put your credit card number on the check. The merchant cannot charge your credit card anyway. Show the card to the merchant if he needs to check for identification.

- Never give your credit card number unless you know the company is definitely legitimate.

- Tear up all your carbons.

- Never give your credit card number over the telephone unless you personally called a legitimate company.

- Ignore mail notices that you won a prize or deals too good to believe. These schemes often have hidden charges or are outright fraud.

- Never give your credit card number to someone who calls to "verify" your number. The person may give you a phony account number and hope you will respond by saying, "No, my number is 222222222."

- Keep track of your blank and voided checks. A criminal can create a phony bank draft if they have access to a blank check. The bank drafts do not require your signature and the only way a bank has of knowing that the draft is phony is if you complain. Discovery may take weeks, and the criminal will have already fled.

You are responsible for protecting yourself. If you do not use all of your credit cards on a regular basis, make a habit of seeing that you still have them. You can do this weekly or biweekly. Think of this as a protection check. Consider purchasing credit card insurance. This will free you of the $50 liability. Additionally, the insurance company will notify all issuers of your credit cards.

Chapter 4

Date Rape

The Date Rapist

Lisa had been dating Jim for two weeks. She had met him at a fraternity party, and tonight was their fourth date. She did not feel totally comfortable with him, but her friends really liked him. He was certainly handsome, but she found him a little too pushy. He often made all the decisions as to where they were going and even what movie they would see.

Dinner tonight was at an expensive restaurant in town and Jim picked up the tab. Jim walked her to her apartment, and Lisa agreed to let him come up for a few minutes to have some tea. Since her apartment was small, she did not have much furniture. They sat side by side on the couch, listening to a jazz record.

Jim put his arm around her, and she slowly pushed it away.

"Jim, I like you, but I think we should take our time," she said softly. He pulled her to him and began to kiss her.

"Please don't," she said. "You're hurting me." Jim did not respond. Now Lisa was really frightened.

"Stop, don't!" she cried. Jim was convinced that she was just playing hard to get. After all, he had heard that one of his friends had "scored" with her on the first date, and this was already Jim's fourth date with Lisa.

Jim "knew" that some women liked it rough. Jim placed his hand over her mouth and threatened her.

Analysis

This chapter is as important for college men as it is for college women. In this story Jim viewed Lisa as just another conquest. He would not have considered his actions rape.

What Is Rape?

Rape is the act of forcing sexual intercourse without the other party's consent. People often believe that rape is committed by a stranger lurking in the dark. However, rape can also be committed by someone known to the victim. This type of rape is referred to as date rape, the act of forcing sex on an acquaintance. Other names for date rape are social rape or cocktail rape. Rape is rape. It is a crime of violence. As soon as the aggressor ignores the victim's refusal and intercourse occurs, even if the couple know one another, rape occurs. In college settings, date rape is common.

Rape is a unique crime because not only is the body violated, but also the victim's entire spirit. Rape victims often face lifetime emotional and physical scars and may be unable to adjust to former lifestyles.

Symptoms of the trauma may include:

- Guilt: The victim often feels guilty for what has happened and thinks that she was responsible. She may think she could have avoided the rape if only she had said something differently or reacted differently. Society may reinforce these ideas by questioning whether she provoked the attack. The victim may be so embarrassed that she never reports the rape, thus letting the perpetrator get away.

- Mistrust: The victim may feel that she can never trust a friend again if she was raped by an acquaintance. She may become unable to carry on normal relationships, especially those with members of the opposite sex. She may be so traumatized that she can no longer relate sexually to her mate. There is always more than one victim in a rape.

• Depression: Guilt may lead to bouts of depression. Studies have shown that women who have been raped are more likely to commit suicide.

• Irrational fear: A rape victim may develop irrational fears, which interfere with her ability to carry on normal social interactions.

Myths of Rape

Many stereotypical images of women exist and are perpetuated in the media and popular entertainment. These images have conditioned people to believe that rape is a crime of passion or caused by promiscuous women. A common phrase is, "If she dresses like that, she is asking for it." Because of the stigma that society attaches to a rape, the victim can expect this attitude from police officers to defense attorneys.

Another sad consequence of rape is that several groups will exploit these myths and "rape" the victim again as they put forward their own social and political agendas. If she is lucky, they may just use her name to sell papers. When a prominent politician's nephew was accused of rape, even respected newspapers such as the *New York Times*, and network television studios broadcasted the alleged victim's name. The *New York Times* even revealed her past sexual history, as if that had any bearing on her accusations.

Prevention

If you are involved in a relationship, make sure that the lines of communication are clear between you and your partner. You must be assertive when it comes to your physical and mental well-being.

Your partner should not be in doubt about your sexual limits, so express them clearly. If you are just getting to know somebody, date in public places or in groups until you know the person. If you feel the situation is going too fast or too far, say so directly. Use phrases such as, "I do not want you to touch me there," as opposed to "I think we are going too fast." When physical action is initiated, name the offending action: "You are hurting my wrist. Let go!" as opposed to "Please, don't." If your date doesn't stop, use defensive tactics to escape.

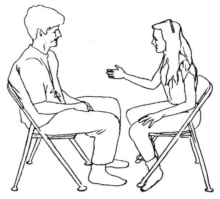

Make sure the lines of communication are clear between you and your partner.

Proper defensive training will teach you to identify the right opportunity to maximize effective resistance. Current literature advocates not resisting if you feel your life is threatened. However, this advice could be fatal in a society where AIDS and other potentially deadly venereal diseases exist.

Many women fear they will be hurt if they resist. Research on avoiding rape by a stranger suggests defensive strategies are an effective avoidance method. A study to examine whether a rape was completed and the victim injured if she resisted was undertaken by Vernon Quinsey and Douglas Upfold. Chance interruptions were removed to isolate cases in which the victim resisted. Data on 95 completed rapes and 41 attempted rapes were analyzed. Survey results yielded:

- If a woman resisted, she did not increase her chance of physical injury.

- Women were more likely to avoid rape when they screamed and yelled for help or physically resisted.

Another study was conducted in 1986 by Joyce Levine MacCombe and Mary Koss to determine effective avoidance strategies for college women ages 18-25. The study included 231 interviews and a survey of 35 avoiders and 47 victims. Differences between the avoiders and the victims included:

- At the time of the assault, the rape avoiders experienced more aggressive emotions.

- The avoiders perceived the assault as less violent.

- The avoiders used active response strategies, such as yelling and physical resistance.

Rape and the Courts

If a rape occurs, the difficulty of proof often falls upon the victim. If no witnesses were present, and the victim froze and no physical violence occurred, the rape will be difficult to prove. If you are assaulted, you must make it obvious that you resisted. The courts will be less likely to deny you if your attacker has scratches and bruises inflicted by you in defense.

Defense attorneys may use several strategies to win an acquittal for their clients. These strategies are often an attempt to discredit and humiliate the victim. They include:

- The victim consented so no rape occurred.

- No sexual assault occurred.

- This is a case of mistaken identity.

- The victim's sexual history or provocative style of dress indicate that she probably invited or consented to the incident.

Rape Awareness

Both men and women should be very concerned about rape and should openly discuss it. Campuses can set up dormitory lectures. Fraternities as well as sororities should set these up to educate their members.

Understand date rape and correct misconceptions held by your friends and associates. A young man should realize that a rape accusation can have lasting effects. His reputation can be tarnished severely, and even if he is vindicated, some people will remain doubtful of his innocence. In this day of information retrieval he can forget about holding any elected positions.

Encourage a friend who has been raped to get a medical examination.

How to Help a Friend Who Has Been Raped

If a friend is raped, you can be a tremendous support. Encourage her to get a physical checkup immediately, and accompany her to the hospital emergency room. Make sure that she takes a change of clothes as police may require her current clothing for evidence. She should not bathe or douche before going to the emergency room. Valuable evidence, such as semen, could be destroyed.

Your friend will be given a pelvic examination and blood tests for venereal disease. Encourage her to seek counseling and offer your complete support. Unfortunately, effects of this incident may be with your friend for a long time, so try to be available for her if she wants to talk. Do a lot of listening and check on her periodically.

Rape Quiz

Answer the following questionnaire to determine how knowledgeable you are about rape. Give the most correct answer.

1)
a) The typical rapist is a stranger lurking in a dark alley.
b) The typical rapist could be anyone, even a family member.
c) The typical rapist comes from a low-income family.

2)
a) Rape is often a crime of passion.
b) Rape is a crime of violence.
c) It is not rape if the victim doesn't resist.

3)
a) Rape has not occurred when a woman plays "hard to get."
b) Sexual intercourse between two strangers is rape.
c) Sexual intercourse without the consent of one partner constitutes rape.

4)
a) Women want to be forced to have sex.
b) Rape has not occurred if the women agrees to have sex.
c) Some women say "no" but really mean "yes" when it comes to sex.

5)
a) Loose women want to get raped.
b) If a woman wears provocative clothing on a date, this is a sign of consent, so you don't need her permission to have sex with her.
c) Consent may be measured in other ways besides a verbal "yes."

6)
a) If a woman is picked up at a bar, her date can legally have sex with her at any time.
b) If a woman is picked up at a fraternity party, her date can legally have sex with her without her consent, but only if they've had sex before.

c) If a woman is picked up at a bar, her date can't have sex with her unless she consents.

7)
a) Any woman can get raped.
b) Only stupid women get raped.
c) Only women who sleep around get raped.

8)
a) One way to avoid a potential date rape is to give in to your date's demands.
b) One way to avoid a potential date rape situation is to never date someone you meet at a party.
c) One way to avoid a potential date rape is to communicate your sexual attitudes clearly to your partner.

9)
a) If a woman is attacked, she should shower immediately to cleanse herself of the incident.
b) If a woman is attacked, she should report the rape immediately to the police.
c) If a woman is attacked, she should go immediately to a hospital.

10)
a) Date rape is a gentler form of rape because the assailant is known.
b) Nothing will happen to a man if he forces a woman to have sex with him and he knows her.
c) Date rape is as hideous as rape by a stranger and can be punished just as harshly.

Answers

1 (b) A date rapist could be anyone. In fact, there is no specific profile. Common myths are that rape only occurs between strangers (a) or that the rapist is easily identifiable because he is poor (c).

2 (b) Rape is a crime of violence. It is a hideous violation of another person's being and can cause lifetime trauma. It is not a crime of passion (a). If a person says "no" and does not resist physically, it is still rape (c).

3 (c) Sexual assault without the consent of a partner is rape. There are no exceptions. If the man thinks that a woman is "playing hard to get" (a), by not giving her consent and the man proceeds, it is still rape. Obviously, sex between two consenting adults is not rape (b).

4 (b) Once again, consent is necessary between two parties. If you answered (a), I suggest you seek counseling. Don't second guess your partner (c). If a woman says "no," that means no.

5 (c) Consent can be measured in other ways besides saying "yes." If a woman disrobes with the intention of having sex with a man, her actions can be viewed as a form of consent. However, she has a right to change her mind at any time. A woman has a right to wear any style of clothing she wants (b). Even if a woman is promiscuous it does not mean that she wants to be raped (a). Even if a man believes that a promiscuous woman or one who dresses provocatively wants to have sex, he cannot assume so.

6 (c) Again, the key word is consent. A man has no automatic right to have sex with a woman without her consent (a), even if he has had sex with her before (b).

7 (a) Any woman can be raped, so prepare to survive such an ordeal. Even brilliant women (b) and pious women (c) are rape victims. The best defense is to avoid the situation through continuous mental and physical training.

8 (c) You must communicate with your partner so that no misunderstandings occur. Giving in to pressure and consenting to have sex is not rape (a). Many great relationships begin at parties (b), just communicate clearly with any partner.

9 (c) If a woman is attacked, she should go immediately to a hospital and get a checkup. She may have suffered more physical injury than she initially thought. She should not change her clothes or wash; incriminating evidence could be destroyed (a). At the hospital, rape counselors will be available and the crime can be reported to the police later (b).

10 (c) Date rape is just as hideous as rape by a stranger and both are equally punishable in the eyes of the law (b) & (c).

Chapter 5

Transportation

Public Transportation

The night was chilly and Ann was glad that she had brought her sorority sweater. She was waiting in a subway station and the train seemed to be taking an extremely long time. Ann hated working nights, but she needed the money to pay for her tuition. Because she had been on this schedule a year without incident, she felt relatively at ease. But she was still wary of traveling late at night and had her Mace ready in her purse.

Ann was concerned about a term paper due tomorrow morning. She knew that tonight she would be up all night. Her thoughts were interrupted when she heard a voice ask, "Do you go to DePaul?"

She looked up and saw a neatly dressed man.

"I'm going to meet a friend at a campus party," he continued. "Could you tell me where I should get off ?"

Ann gave him directions. The stranger continued to make small talk. When the train came, she entered a car and sat down next to a window. He followed her and sat down next to her. Ann felt uncomfortable, but since the stranger had not done anything wrong, she did not want to seem rude. She did not object.

Then the stranger put his hand on Ann's knee. She was terrified and her vocal chords froze, but she pushed his hand away. She thought briefly of the Mace, but ruled it out. She knew that she could not get it out of her purse quickly enough. The stranger continued to caress her knee. When the conductor entered the car to collect the tickets, the stranger quickly stood up. Ann was crying and passengers looked at her, but no one tried to find out why she was distressed. Meanwhile, the stranger exited, looked back at Ann, and winked.

Analysis

Ann could have done several things that might have helped her avoid this encounter. Ann was in the white state, oblivious to her surroundings. Just because nothing had happened for a year, she had been lulled into a sense of security. If a violent crime happens to you, statistics are irrelevant. Many students think, "It couldn't happen to me." Well, it could! At night, no one should be able to walk up to you unnoticed. When on the train, your state according to our color code should be orange. Sleeping is not a good idea as it leaves you too exposed.

For the most part you have the right to dress any way you want and to go wherever you want, at any time you want. But it is wise, if you use public transportation, to wear nondescript clothing. A person should not be able to accurately guess details about you, especially your destination, from your appearance.

There is safety in numbers, so stand next to a group of people. Courtesy is appropriate if you are asked directions. However, if you are not comfortable with making small talk, silence is the best way to confront the situation. Give short answers and walk away if necessary.

If you want to lose somebody when you enter a subway, wait for him to enter a car and then go to another one. If he follows, keep moving until you are in a car with a conductor. If the person threatens you in any way, embarrass him in a loud voice. Say that you do not know him. Call attention to the situation.

As soon as someone deliberately tries to harass you sexually, the best way to get rid of him is to embarrass him. Perverts are often cowards and they don't want to attract attention. Do not be timid, as your unwillingness to resist is an assailant's form of control in this situation. Decent people may try to help you; unfortunately, you cannot rely on others, so be prepared to back up your vocal demands with defensive tactics.

If you must travel during nonbusy hours, consider traveling with a friend or acquaintance. When you are waiting for public transportation, stand near the token booth or under a light. Because crime against public transportation passengers is such a problem, police often pass by these areas and look specifically at these spots.

Be alert to schedule changes, express service, and route changes due to construction. If you are not absolutely sure that a bus or train goes to your destination at a certain time, call the public transportation organization or ask the driver or conductor.

Two female college students went to see a movie one night in downtown Chicago. They traveled on the subway, with which they were both familiar. However, due to construction, the route was changed and the train went express to a rough neighborhood. Luckily, they boarded another train that went express back to downtown Chicago. They were shaken up and missed their movie, but were relieved to get back safely to campus.

Know your destination. If you don't know the exact route, call the public transportation organization. If you act as if you are unfamiliar with public transportation, a criminal might mark you as a potential victim. So always act as if you know where you are going.

If the stops are not announced, tell the driver or conductor your destination and ask him to let you know when you should get off. All public transportation drivers have two-way radios, so stay close to the driver of the vehicle. If you witness a crime and you hail a bus driver, he can help you by calling the police.

Stand back from the tracks or away from the curb to avoid being pushed in front of an oncoming vehicle. This type of crime occurs every year in the United States.

When choosing a seat on the subway, if the seats are arranged in pairs, always try to sit in an aisle seat so you can beat a hasty retreat if necessary. Choose an aisle seat even if you sit by yourself. You can always let someone sit by the window.

If the seats are arranged along the side of the wall, and someone undesirable is standing in front of you, get up and move.

Sitting next to an exit is unwise, as many purse snatchers or pickpockets wait for the train to stop and then grab your jewelry or purse. You could run off the train after the individual, but he may have accomplices or you may exit into an area that is not familiar. A better course of action is to stay on the train and report the crime later when you reach an area you know is safe.

Rifling through your purse for fare is not a good idea. Have your fare in hand. Use tokens or exact fare when possible. You do not want to expose the fact that you have additional money by receiving change and then revealing where you keep the rest of your money. If you have fare, separate it from the rest of your money and place any change directly in your pocket.

Think defensively. Always carry your wallet in a coat pocket or your front pants pocket because pickpockets often slash back pants pockets with a razor. You don't feel anything, but the wallet falls out easily. Even zipping shut your backpack pocket does not protect your valuables from a pickpocket. Pickpockets work with accomplices. So if someone bumps into you and you find your wallet missing, even if you accost the original pickpocket, you probably will not recover your wallet as the pickpocket has already passed it on to an accomplice. Also remember that if a physical confrontation occurs, you may have to face accomplices, too.

Purses should be carried under the arm like a football. Handbags with straps should be carried over your shoulder and not over your neck so that if your handbag is snatched, you are not pulled, as well.

If you suspect someone might follow you from a bus or train, don't gather up your purse or packages before the stop. Wait until the last minute to get off.

Amazingly, despite witnesses, many crimes are committed against public transportation passengers. These crimes include assault, criminal sexual assault, indecent exposure, armed robbery, and pickpocketing.

Recently a law enforcement officer told me he witnessed a chain snatching on a subway. He was in civilian clothing, therefore the thief was not deterred by his presence. The officer immediately followed the assailant and demanded that he return the victim's chain. Interestingly, the assailant stopped running as soon as he got off the train because he wasn't expecting anybody to follow him.

The thief was surprised to actually be challenged. He was uncooperative even after the police officer identified himself. As soon as the officer drew his gun, the thief changed his attitude. He emptied his pockets, which contained several chains, and returned the chain he had just stolen. The woman who had been robbed did not want to press charges, so the thief was released.

Physical injury can occur if jewelry is suddenly snatched, so try to conceal it. Turn the stone on all your rings to the inside of your finger so that the stone isn't showing. Any medallions or pendants should be tucked into your shirt or blouse, out of sight. A watch should be covered with your sleeve or placed in your pocket. Expensive-looking or large earrings should be put in your pocket. Do not attract unwanted attention and practice your skills of invisibility, such as avoiding prolonged eye contact.

Rifling through your wallet in public for fare is not a good idea.

Remember, defensive tactics are a last resort. If you are robbed, give up your money. If you must carry large amounts of cash, carry it in a money belt or nontraditional place, such as a sock. A thief has no time to search you thoroughly. Leave some money in your wallet so that the thief will be happy with his loot, and his attention will be diverted from you.

Before coming to college, write to the public transportation organization to request schedules. Make sure you get current schedules after you arrive. If you've never taken public transportation, ask someone who has experience to ride with you the first time. He can show you how to request stops, where to pay, and where to board.

Personal Transportation

The sun had just set as Jeff hopped into his car. Jeff was about 10 minutes late for his appointment with his academic advisor. He glanced at his dashboard and saw that his gas tank was on empty, as usual, and he was going about 10 miles per hour over the speed limit. Jeff knew that to stop for gas now would make him unbearably late, so he was willing to risk driving with virtually no fuel.

Jeff weaved in and out of traffic. Some angry motorists honked at him. The driver of one sedan that he cut off began to blink his headlights. Jeff ignored the sedan and continued to weave in and out. Only after he turned a corner did he notice that the sedan was chasing him.

Jeff became frightened. Recent reports of angry motorists shooting at each other in Los Angeles raced through his head. He looked back, but the other car had no front plates, and because its headlights were on, he could not see the driver's face.

Suddenly Jeff's car sputtered. He realized with horror that he was out of gas. He pulled to the side of the road. The sedan pulled right behind him. Jeff grabbed the baseball bat he kept in his car. Jeff immediately opened his car door and stepped out, bat in hand, and charged toward the other driver's car.

"I'm an off-duty police officer," the burly man said, flashing his badge. "You better put that bat away before you get yourself in more trouble."

Analysis

Jeff's first mistake was improper car maintenance. Many college students drive old cars because they are affordable. When money is tight, comfort is often of secondary concern and students often maintain their own automobiles.

In choosing a car, make sure that the car is reliable. If the car is unreliable, make sure that you know the car's limitations. In other words, if a mechanic you trust tells you that your car's clutch is in bad condition and will only last another 200 miles, do not drive more than 200 miles and have the clutch replaced immediately.

Proper vehicular safety begins before you even enter your car. You should know the rudiments of caring for your car. Almost all cars have an owner's handbook that can be purchased inexpensively from any auto shop or car dealership. The car should receive regular oil changes and maintenance checks to minimize possible expensive and/or life-threatening surprises.

You should never allow your car to run out of gas. You should know your tank's capacity. Always keep your car on at least a quarter of a tank. If you want to find out the limit of your car's tank, drive around a campus parking lot with a funnel and a couple of gallons of gas in an appropriate container. When you run out of gas, notice the needle's position. If you do this, I do not recommend that you try it at night, and only do so on a well-lighted and well-traveled route with a friend.

When approaching your parked car, you should first look around to see if anyone is standing by it. Make a complete circle around the car so that you can check all sides and underneath before entering. Your keys should be in your hand to avoid fumbling for them. Look in the back seat and front seat, and pivot 180 degrees before entering. If your car doesn't start, keep in mind that it could have been sabotaged if you have an exterior hood release. Be wary of unsolicited offers of help.

Many students carry a club or a knife in their car for protection, but such weapons can only lead to trouble. Most of these people don't know how or when to use a weapon efficiently. Often the weapon is turned against them. In the eyes of the law, if you draw a weapon, you have escalated the situation. Angry words may now lead to a fight causing death or injury.

When driving, your doors should be locked at all times and the windows rolled up. When Jeff pulled over, he should have remained in his car with his windows rolled up and doors locked until the man properly identified himself. Additionally, Jeff should have sounded his horn as long as the man continued to be perceived as a threat.

Closed windows are also protection against a thief waiting for someone to stop at a stoplight and then snatching a purse off the front seat or a watch off a rider's hand. Purses or bags should be placed under your seat.

If you believe that you are being followed, you should drive to the nearest police or fire station. If you do not know their location, drive to a crowded gas station, where you can get out and phone the police. You can also continuously honk your horn to attract attention to your predicament.

If you are traveling on a deserted road and are bumped, continue to drive until you reach the nearest police station. Then you can give the information to the police. In some cases, accidents have been caused intentionally. When the drivers got out of their cars to exchange insurance information, the person who caused the accident attacked the other driver.

While you are driving, never pick up hitchhikers. One common ploy is for a woman to appear to be in distress. When you stop, you are jumped by multiple accomplices. If a legitimate emergency arises, drive to the nearest phone and call the police. Never get out of the car.

Deaths have been caused by people hurling rocks at cars from overpasses, so be wary of unusual activity on an overpass.

If you get a flat tire, drive on until you reach a well-lighted and well-traveled area. Rims can be replaced; for that matter, the entire car can be replaced, so think safety first. If your car breaks down, put up the hood and tie a white cloth to the antenna. Get back in your car, put on your flashers, roll up the windows, and lock the doors.

Traveling with flares and an extra blanket in the car is also a good strategy, depending on the climate. Passing motorists as well as police will recognize flares as a symbol of distress. If someone stops to help, ask the person to call the police for you without getting out of the car. I recommend declining offers of help to fix the car. You cannot run the risk of exposing yourself to a stranger's intervention.

Commuting students should carpool as often as possible for greater security. Find out if your campus has groups for commuting students. If there is no commuting group, start one.

Here are some ideas to implement when planning or evaluating your current car pool:

- Make sure that all of the drivers in your car pool have valid drivers licenses and safe driving records. This can be accomplished with the help of the campus department of public safety.

- All drivers in your car pool should be current students registered for the quarter or semester. The drivers can also be faculty or staff member. The point is that the person should have a legitimate reason for making the trip.

- Any cars in the pool should be properly registered, inspected, and well maintained to lessen the chances of mechanical failure while in route.

- A regularly updated schedule should be located at the student affairs office so that all participants are aware if the schedule changes.

Chapter 6

Drugs and Alcohol

The Party

Skip fell backward and his chair crashed to the floor. The whole party roared with laughter. Loud rock-and-roll music blared through the fraternity. Clouds of marijuana smoke drifted through the air. Skip was the last of the pledges to fall. By the brothers' calculation, he had drunk two 16-ounce bottles of straight whiskey without vomiting.

The other pledges were lying about the room, groaning and slightly comatose. Skip was not moving, but the brothers were not overly concerned. After all, they had all undergone the same ritual and nobody in their fraternity had ever awakened with more than a severe hangover and a bruised ego.

Biff was the most sober of the lot. He soon noticed that Skip was not moaning or groaning. In fact, Skip did not appear to be breathing at all. Biff went over to Skip and watched him closely. Skip's chest did not seem to be moving. Biff felt for a pulse, first on the neck and next on the wrist. Biff could find it on neither.

"Hey guys, I don't think Skip is okay," he said.

"Oh, he's all right. Just splash some water on him," said one of the seniors.

When the water did not revive Skip, the mood became somber. The brothers knew that since Skip was below 21, the fraternity would probably be placed on housing probation. Reluctantly, they called 911.

Analysis

Most colleges publicly discourage hazing. Yet because of the difficulty of enforcing the policy, private rituals for new members still occur. Skip's story is typical and not the sole domain of fraternities. Often alcohol is used by other groups to initiate new members. The intention is to have a good time and a few laughs and for the initiate to share in the pain of recovery, which is supposed to make the initiate closer and more dedicated to the group.

Freshmen, in particular, are very vulnerable to this practice because they want to impress their new friends. Unfortunately, they often use excessive amounts of alcohol or drugs and they have no idea how the substances will adversely affect them. Upperclassmen, who have a moral obligation for the welfare of new initiates, often have no idea of the full legal consequences they may face if one of their members is seriously injured. Skip's fraternity brothers were only worried about housing probation. They did not realize that they could be sent to jail for negligent homicide or face civil suits from Skip's parents.

Many college students will experiment with alcohol or drugs, which can alter their state of awareness. The purpose of this chapter is to provide an understanding of the legal consequences of drugs in relation to a college setting, crime and substance abuse, and how to conduct yourself in the presence of illegal drugs.

Legal Consequences

Drug and alcohol use may seem casual on campus, but students must be aware of possible legal consequences associated with their use. A whole group in the presence of substance abuse may pay the penalty. A campus organization could be disbanded or put on probation because of a few people's actions. Or an arrest could mean embarrassment and cost time and money.

- Twelve members of a lacrosse team in Illinois were indicted on criminal charges after a member died at an initiation party. The student had consumed a large quantity of alcohol. Although the students were acquitted of criminal charges, they were charged with a civil wrongful death lawsuit and a misdemeanor charge of delivering alcohol to a minor. The case is still pending and the students, if convicted, face up to 364 days in jail and a $1,000 fine. In addition, each student was suspended from the university. Think of how many times you could have been involved in such a situation.

- At Oberlin University, one student grew marijuana plants in his room and left them there over spring break. The plants were discovered by a university official and as a result, all roommates were charged with misdemeanors and suspended from the university.

- At the University of Virginia, three fraternity houses were raided by the police for running a narcotics ring. Eleven students were arrested and due to the national media attention, the school's reputation was tarnished.

If you are arrested, you may think that you will get off with a suspended sentence and that it is no big deal. But the long-term ramifications can be severe. Many professional organizations will not certify you if you have a drug conviction. Your future employment also will be threatened if your criminal record is exposed. Many companies simply will not hire you. In this day of easy information access, you can be certain that you will have difficulty ever being voted into public office. If you are a foreign student, you can be deported and lose rights to ever enter the United States again.

Here are a few suggestions for groups who serve alcohol:

- Designate a referee. This person should be the dedicated nondrinker during the party who decides when people have had enough to drink. The referee should be trained in CPR and first aid. This duty can be rotated among the members.

• Designate a driver. This individual also should not drink at the event and should maintain control of car keys or cab fares.

• Designate a holder of the keys. Anybody who is invited to your party should not be allowed to drive home drunk. You have a moral responsibility for your guests as well as the legal liability associated with letting someone drive drunk from your party. The holder is not allowed to drink during the party. If anybody is too incapacitated, the holder is responsible for seeing that he gets safe passage home.

• Disallow illegal drugs in your dwellings. This rule should be enforced so that the whole group does not suffer for one person's actions.

• Observe the 21-year-old drinking age. If word of underage drinking at your party leaks out, the college may seek disciplinary action against the party's organizers, even if no injuries occur. If injuries do occur, make sure that you are not contributing to the delinquency of a minor.

• Serve low-alcohol drinks. Some brands of nonalcoholic beer and wines as well as virgin drinks can be served.

Here are some tips to protect yourself if you are in a place where alcohol is served:

• If a drunk hassles you, don't go outside alone. Complain to the bartender or call a cab or a friend. Do not hesitate to use defensive tactics if you are followed outside.

• Stay away from the punch. You have no way of knowing the alcohol content or if it was laced with drugs.

• If you are drinking alcohol, drink from a bottle or can

that you opened. Even if you watch someone make a drink for you, you may not notice if something is slipped into the drink, especially if you have been drinking.

- Discard your drink if it has been out of your sight. If you get up to dance and leave your drink on the table, don't drink from it. You do not know if someone might have slipped something into it.

- If you realize that someone has put drugs into your drink, have a friend take you to the emergency room immediately.

- Pay for your drinks in small bills. Do not attract undue attention to yourself by paying for them in large bills. Criminals often hang out at bars looking for victims too inebriated to defend themselves.

Crime and Substance Abuse

Illegal drugs are a dangerous business. You can risk physical injury from dealers, loan sharks, and others involved in the drug trade. Not surprisingly, alcohol and drug abuse are present in many violent crimes. Criminals will choose victims under the influence because the criminals know that the victims cannot react to defend themselves. Let's review our criteria for potential victims and relate those characteristics to someone under the influence of alcohol or drugs:

- **Demeanor.** It is obvious when someone has had too much to drink. His motor control is impaired, so he often sways when standing or does not walk in straight lines. Alcohol is a relaxant and a completely inebriated person has difficultly looking alert. Drugs such as amphetamines or cocaine will make a person appear more aggressive or as if they have excessive energy. He may walk too fast or erratically and continuously repeat motions, such as grinding his teeth or tapping his toes.

- **Eye communication.** An individual under the influence will have difficulty concentrating and maintaining eye contact. His dull gaze can indicate to would-be attackers that he is not alert and easy prey.

- **Gestures and facial expressions.** Someone under the influence may not be able to control his facial expressions, depending on the drug. Also, puffiness and redness of the face are indicators to an attacker that the intended victim is not at full defensive capacity.

- **Outer voice.** Breath control is difficult for someone under the influence. Loss of breath control may affect his voice and cause cracking, which may alert the aggressor that the intended victim is frightened. The drugs may also give someone false bravado, which can cause him to challenge the aggressor. The aggressor could call the intended victim's bluff, knowing that he cannot respond.

- **Inner voice.** If you are under the influence your ability to concentrate is impaired and you may not be able to trust your inner voice.

Be wary of anything that causes you to lose your sense of control. If you are under the influence, your ability to assess a potentially violent situation is impaired.

How to Conduct Yourself in the Presence of Illicit Drugs

Tolerance is not the better part of common sense when illegal substances are involved. If you see substance abuse or drug paraphernalia, leave the vicinity. The old saying "Two heads are better than one" is often inaccurate. Avoid becoming a victim of what behavioral scientists call group think.

Group think involves members of a group who make a decision because of peer pressure, ignoring risk and alternative courses of action. These members believe that they are invulnerable to harm because the group

"Bong"

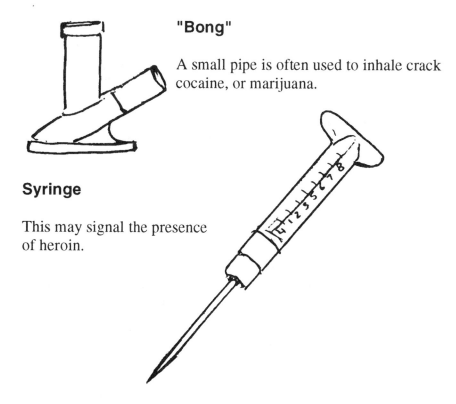

A small pipe is often used to inhale crack cocaine, or marijuana.

Syringe

This may signal the presence of heroin.

Mirror

A small mirror is often used to provide a smoothe surface to inhale cocaine.

Alligator Clip

Also called a roach clip. This device is often used to assist in inhaling marijuana.

made a decision, such as a decision to hold hazings. These members also rationalize group decisions. They think that because everybody else is doing something, drugs for example, why shouldn't they? They also view their own drug use as harmless, although they would condemn drug abuse that leads to violent crime. People who question the use of narcotics are sometimes ridiculed or made to feel they let the group down. Those who don't speak up are assumed to be in accordance with the group's actions.

You can protect yourself against group think by practicing the following steps:

- Be risk averse: When your personal safety is involved, always think of things in terms of "What am I going to lose if I do this?" as opposed to "What am I going to gain?" As always, you are responsible for your own safety.

- Speak up: If you do not agree with allowing illicit drugs in the group, speak up. You may be surprised at the number of allies you may have. Never underestimate your influence. Many people have similar attitudes, but they may be unwilling to come forward first.

- Support others who speak up: There is strength in numbers and you can turn group think to your advantage.

- Be direct in your objections: Point out exactly what you see as potential problems and the inherent dangers of drug and alcohol abuse.

- Walk away: If you cannot in good conscience support the decision of a group, say clearly why you don't agree and walk away.

Promote drug and alcohol awareness through campus dormitory chats. Take a mature and safe attitude in your partying.

Chapter 7

Vacation

The Hitchhiker

Susan just loved the English countryside. She regretted that she would have to return home to Los Angeles in a few days to start her final semester. This trip had been the best vacation ever. She had hitchhiked her way across much of Europe on a small budget, staying in youth hostels.

She especially enjoyed England because her heritage was English. She would never consider hitchhiking at home, but here everything seemed so peaceful and so safe. When a middle-aged man passed her going in the opposite direction, she was surprised to see him stop and make a U-turn. He pulled up beside her, and asked, "May I offer you a lift, young lady?"

"Sure," she said, "but aren't you going out of your way?"

"Oh, I'm retired now and I have all the time in the world." She got in the front seat, thinking to herself that people were certainly friendly.

They drove along and he talked about art museums, famous sights, and fine wine. She enjoyed the conversation, impressed by his knowledge. They took a turn and Susan noticed a road sign saying that her destination was in the opposite direction.

"Wasn't that our turn?" asked Susan, thinking he had made a mistake.

"Oh, I've lived here all my life and I know a shortcut that can save us miles," replied the driver.

Suddenly he swerved to the side of the road. Susan's head hit the dashboard. She tried to grab the handle of the door and for the first time, noticed that it wasn't there.

Analysis

Many students go on vacation to foreign countries. They want to make new friends and experience other cultures. Do not completely drop your guard when you travel. Stay in the yellow state. Susan's critical mistake was her attitude in assuming that just because she was on vacation and away from urban crime, she did not need to be concerned about her safety. Every country has its share of criminals or sociopaths, even in the tiniest island in the Caribbean. Keep in mind that tourism literature never mentions the negatives of a country, such as its crime rate against tourists.

This carefree attitude is prevalent among college students. On several occasions when I was an undergraduate, other students who knew that I was from the Caribbean would tell me of their plans to visit the area. When I asked where they were staying, I was often shocked at the answer: They had no plans, but figured that they would stay on a beach. I would like to think that I saved some inconvenience by directing them elsewhere.

Try not to leave your common sense at home. In a foreign country people may indeed appear friendlier because they are reliant on tourist dollars. Some of them may be friendlier, some of them may not. These are people just like those in your country, and with that knowledge, realize you could encounter similar problems.

If you concur that sexist attitudes exist in the United States where women are legally treated as equals, think of the attitudes that exist where women have substantially restricted roles. Another surprise, which may not be evident, is that many people in other countries consider Americans lazy, stupid, wealthy, and loose. If this attitude is combined with a mind that has a criminal bent, you can count on being considered a target.

Ignore the myth of the ignorant foreigner. Even if you are in a less-developed region, chances are that the people you meet are as intelligent as you are. If you think you're getting an unbelievable bargain, you probably aren't. Actually, you are even more susceptible to common cons because the perpetrator knows that you may be too embarrassed to report it.

Hitchhiking

I strongly recommend that you not hitchhike because you can find many low-cost travel alternatives to seeking rides with complete strangers. If you do hitchhike:

There are several cheap alternatives to hitchiking.

- Never take a lift from someone who changes direction to pick you up. He may have some alterior motive. Most students would become suspicious if they were in a similar situation on the streets of Chicago. Always think defensively!

- Before entering a vehicle, make a mental note of the license plate number and the color and make of the car. Most things that people forget are things they never looked at in detail. If necessary, you may be able to recall such details through hypnosis. Look in the back seat to see if anybody might be hiding there. Be particularly suspicious if you see tarps that appear to be covering equipment.

• Once inside, check to see that the door handle and windows work. Door handles are sometimes made nonfunctional to prevent you from exiting. Test a door's handle by first closing the door lightly, then reopen it to close it harder. If the door jams when you first close it lightly, it will be easier to force open because it is not completely shut. This tactic is also a nonoffensive gesture as people often do not close a door properly the first time. Roll down a window slightly so you can yell for help if necessary. Rolling it down completely can help you escape.

• Make sure that you know your destination. A basic understanding of how to read a map is a necessity. If you are in a country where you don't speak the language, learn how to pronounce your destination the way the natives say it so you can avoid honest mistakes. Take a pen and mark areas on the map that you want to avoid. Often a native of the area, such as a tour guide, a desk clerk, or a police officer will be very helpful in telling you where not to go. Exploring is part of the fun of foreign travel, but can have fatal consequences. Recently in Mexico, two students looking for a party walked into a drug deal. They were mistaken for Drug Enforcement Agency officials, and were subsequently tortured and executed.

• Never get into a car with two or more adult males. If possible, ride with a family or a female driver. If you notice that the driver's speech is slurred, or he acts in a way that causes you to doubt his intentions or driving ability, get out as soon as you can.

• Accept rides from trusted people in your age group with whom you spent time at a youth hostel.

• Review your defensive options in advance if you suspect possible violence. Think of natural weapons such as the car's dashboard, or a pen, which might be employed for defensive tactics.

Several cheap alternatives to hitchhiking include:

- Varying length passes: These are often available at student discounts. They are used for subways, buses, trains, ferries, airplanes, and combinations of the above. Familiarize yourself with the associated rules of transportation.

A friend of mine was on a train in Yugoslavia. She had her Eurail pass but she had not paid the surcharge to travel there. She tried to pay the additional charge at a station office, but the attendants misunderstood her and only gave her a reservation. The price for the surcharge should have been $2 - $3. However, because she bought it on the train, the conductor demanded $20. She felt ripped off, but she did not know what would happen if she refused, so she paid.

- Consider renting bicycles or mopeds.

The story focused on a hitchhiking incident, but of course other issues are involved in vacation travel. You should conduct yourself with the same mental awareness as you would when you are at home and take the same precautions as you would on the streets at home. And when choosing a place to stay, apply the same criteria to evaluate its security as you would your home.

Traveling Suggestions

When planning your trip, be sure to have a regular point of contact at home. If you revise your route, notify your contact. If you are really in trouble, you want someone to be able to track you and send help if necessary. Also, don't be cruel to your loved ones by neglecting to let them know your whereabouts and whether you are okay.

Arrive at each new destination in daylight. Youth hostels close for the evening and you may get stranded at a train station if currency exchanges are closed.

Read about the places you plan to visit. Familiarize yourself with the local customs and laws. Obey the laws of the foreign country. Do not assume they are the same as those in the United States. Some countries have severe penalties for drug traffickers, so avoid carrying things that can be misinterpreted for drugs, such as little plastic pouches for powder laundry detergent. Always pack your own bags and don't carry anybody's bag for him. You may be carrying contraband without your knowledge.

If you plan to travel to a place where the culture will be very different and disorienting, travel with a group or a friend. Even if you wish to explore alone, you can always split up occasionally.

If you travel, have a regular point of contact at home.

Keep your travel documents with you at all times. Before traveling, make a photocopy of your passport and leave it with your contact. United States passports are worth a premium on most foreign black markets. Also photocopy your airline tickets; losing travel documents can be quite inconvenient.

How to Handle Your Money

Learn local currencies. If you know which countries you are going to visit, obtain a small amount of the foreign currencies from a U.S. bank before you leave. Some banks stock foreign currencies and can order those that they do not have. Before you travel, get an idea of the current exchange rate. Many of these are printed in the business section of most newspapers. Carry a calculator. Unscrupulous exchange employees may try to take advantage of you, particularly if you don't know the language.

Separate your local currency and U.S. currency. Keep your U.S. currency and travel documents in a money belt. Don't flash U.S. dollars as you may be inviting trouble. United States currency is often highly prized, particularly in Eastern bloc countries.

Use traveler's checks and credit cards wherever possible. These are safer than cash and easier to report as stolen.

Vacation Residence

Some additional precautions that you can take with your vacation residence are to sleep with a chair under the doorknob, or to move a piece of furniture next to the door. Lock doors and windows accessible from the outside.

You should know where all fire and emergency exits are located and how to get help immediately. As importantly, you should know who to ask for help. Find out what a legitimate law enforcement uniform looks like. This knowledge will also help you avoid being conned.

If you are not intending to stay in single rooms at night, leave all your valuables and jewelry at home. Hostels usually lock down for the day, but everybody's valuables are often locked together. If others arrive before you, they could steal your possessions.

Home Security While Away

A unique issue to vacation travel is the security of your uninhabited home. Most colleges will hold your mail for you if you live on campus. If you live off campus, however, you must notify the post office to hold your mail. Another alternative is to have a friend pick up your mail and check on your apartment at regular intervals. If you subscribe to a newspaper, cancel the delivery for the duration of your trip so as not to alert someone to your absence.

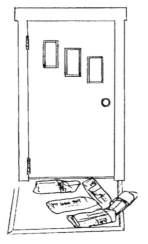

Uncollected newspapers on a doorstep tell a thief that nobody is at home.

If you are going to be gone for more than a week or two, make sure your residence is properly maintained. Lawns should be mowed or snow shoveled regularly. Cars should be locked in a garage or, if left on the street, moved regularly. The appearance that you are still present must be maintained.

Any valuable items should be stored in safety deposit boxes or if the item is too large, leave it with a friend who is also safety-conscious. For example, most friends would gladly check up on your residence every once in a while if you let them use your stereo.

Turn down your telephone ringer and your answering machine so the constant ringing will not alert people that you are not home. On your answering machine message do not indicate that you are on vacation. In fact, do not boast about your vacation so that everybody knows. Some people are even stupid enough to put announcements in the local newspapers about upcoming trips.

When I was a graduate student and living off campus, I foolishly told a neighbor that I would be taking a trip to England. I ran into the man as I was carrying my suitcase to my car the night before I was to leave. He asked in a loud voice, "Oh, so how long are you going to be gone to England? "

I recommend packing and loading your car at the last possible moment and avoid as many people as possible when leaving.

Timed lights and radios are a good way to make someone think that you are home when you aren't.

You should notify your local police of your absence and give them the name of any housesitters that you have or anybody that may have keys to your apartment. Do not hide the keys in a place such as under the front mat or near a potted plant, because a criminal will be expecting people to hide keys in obvious places.

Chapter 8

Common Cons

This chapter deals with common cons that can potentially escalate to violence because you are in close physical proximity to the con artists. Be careful, if you identify a con, do not reveal that you recognize it. Simply refuse the offer and walk away. You can report it later. Anyone who will con people is capable of physically assaulting them. The following scenarios illustrate common cons.

The Bank Examiner

Stan had just deposited his biweekly paycheck. He felt a sense of relief as he knew that he would be able to finance next quarter's tuition with money he made from overtime. As he walked back to the parking lot, he noticed a middle-aged man walking toward him.

The man looked like a stereotypical banker, well-groomed and wearing an impeccable suit. Stan had noticed him standing in the lobby of the bank earlier when he had filled out his deposit receipt.

"Excuse me, young man," said the man. "May I have a minute of your time?"

"How can I help you?" replied Stan, curious as to why the man was stopping him.

"My name is Fred Viloan and I am a vice president of the bank." He handed Stan a business card.

"How would you like to earn a low-interest loan for helping the bank resolve a problem?"

Now Stan's interest was really piqued. He could use the money and helping a bank would look good on his resume. The man continued, "We suspect that one of the tellers has been passing counterfeit money and stealing real money from the bank. We could not ask your help in the bank because the teller might become suspicious."

"What would you like me to do?" asked Stan.

"We want you to withdraw $500 in cash from your savings account and give the money to me out here so that I can check the serial numbers."

The request seemed reasonable, so Stan did as he was asked. Mr. Viloan told him to call the bank in about three hours and ask for him. Stan could then come in and sign for the loan.

Three hours later Stan called the bank. They had never heard of Fred Viloan. Stan never saw his money again.

Analysis

This con appears in many different forms. For example, in one variation, a police officer approaches you. No legitimate company or official would ever request you to take money out of your private accounts.

Do not let your courtesy blind your common sense. If you are ever approached in this manner, just politely refuse the request and continue on your way. Immediately afterward, contact the police to report the incident.

Do not be swayed by physical appearance. Biases allow con artists to manipulate their victims. Stan knew that a bank examiner probably would not approach a customer in a parking lot,

Do not be swayed by physical appearance.

yet Stan only evaluated the superficial evidence, such as the "bank examiner's" appearance and a business card. Stan ignored the unusualness of the situation and the lack of written guarantees. Business cards are quite cheap and very easy to purchase.

Many people would never tell their friends how much money they make or their current state of finances, but would give this information quickly on a form, or to an individual who appears legitimate. Do not be swayed by the appearance of legitimacy. If something does not seem right, trust your intuition.

If you fill out personal information, be careful of who is looking over your shoulder. Do not leave this information in a public place. If you make a mistake on a form and have to dispose of it, tear it up first.

The Pigeon Drop

Nicole waited patiently in line at the bank to use the Automated Teller Machine. She was always careful not to let the person behind her see her identification numbers as she entered them. Before she made her transaction she requested a balance.

Nicole withdrew $40, pocketed the money, and then went to the bus stop. She sat on a bench next to a neatly dressed woman. When Nicole's head was turned, the woman got up and left a brown paper bag on the bench. A slim young woman then sat next to Nicole.

"Is this your paper bag?" the woman inquired.

"No," said Nicole, "I think it belongs to the woman who was sitting here before you."

"Well, she's gone," said the woman, opening the bag.

"Oh, my God! This bag is full of money!" cried the woman.

The first woman was nowhere to be found, so Nicole and the young woman discussed what they should do.

"My lawyer would know the answer," suggested the woman. The two called the lawyer. He said that they should wait a few days to see if the woman came back and if she didn't, they could split the money.

The lawyer agreed to meet them. When he arrived they further agreed that the lawyer would hold the money. To ensure that Nicole and the other woman didn't tell anyone about the money, he asked each to put up some of their own money.

"This bag is full of money!" cried the woman.

Names and addresses were exchanged. When Nicole did not hear from the lawyer after several days, she called the phone number she had been given. It was a false number.

Analysis

Look, you've heard it before, nothing is free. This is a common scam in which the original woman sitting next to Nicole, the second young woman, and the "lawyer" were working together. Their intention was to take Nicole's good faith money and share it.

The bag probably contained no money. If a situation appears too good to be true, it probably is. Turning money over to strangers is foolhardy, even if they appear legitimate. Uniforms are easy to obtain and credentials are easily forged.

Con men often present something that is secret or slightly illegal to an innocent person. Because secrecy is involved the victim is reluctant to reveal it. Even after the victim realizes he has been scammed, he feels foolish and often will not report the crime.

Con artists can manipulate their victims because they know people are profit-seeking and they talk in terms of gains as opposed to losses. For example, in the pigeon drop everything was phrased in terms of the possible monetary gain, as opposed to paying money to get money.

The Woman and the Child

Harry heard a knock on the front door and looked through his peephole. He could see an attractive woman and a child about 8 years old standing in his hallway.

"How can I help you?"

"Hi, my church is offering a free subscription to Sports Illustrated if you'll just fill out this questionnaire."

Harry opened the door and let in the woman and child. He invited them to sit down. The woman began to ask Harry some basic questions such as name and address. The child sat next to her and was well-behaved.

"Do you mind if my child uses your bathroom?" asked the woman.

"Sure, it's right down the hallway to the left," Harry replied.

The woman continued asking Harry questions until the child returned. The woman assured Harry he would receive his free subscription in a couple of weeks. She then thanked him for his time and left.

Later when Harry was going out for the evening, he could not find any of his jewelry or his wallet. Only then did he realize that the child had probably taken them.

Con artists often use a child as an accomplice. A child will give the appearance of legitimacy or is less likely to be suspected. Do not be fooled by such acts. The first hint that this was a con was that Harry would receive a free magazine subscription of considerable value for nothing.

Con artists often use a child as an accomplice.

The woman distracted Harry with the questionnaire while the child stole his possessions. One precaution Harry could have taken was to obtain the name and number of the organization that the woman represented without letting her in. He could have then verified the organization through the phone book, and called the number listed in the directory to see if such a deal was being offered.

Religion is also regularly used in cons. The con artists attempt to gain your trust and increase their legitimacy. When con artists associate themselves with legitimate religions and use titles, such as minister, some people may naturally lower their guards.

Another ploy con artists use is the "rule of reciprocity." That is, they will do you a favor unasked, and expect you to do them a bigger favor later. Of course you feel obliged because the person has done something for you, which was the case when the woman offered something for free and asked Harry for a favor.

The Shell Game

The thin man went into the subway and got on a train. He carried a cardboard sheet under his arm and three bottle tops and a small red ball in his hand.

"Come on, I'll pay 20 bucks to the person who can guess which bottle top this red ball is under," said the thin man, challenging the passengers. He sat down, placed the cardboard sheet on his lap, and began to move the bottle tops so that each time he hid the red ball under one of them.

"I'll play," said a bearded man and he sat in front of the thin man. Everybody could see how slowly the thin man moved the bottle tops and guessing the location of the ball was not difficult. The bearded man won easily.

Jack was on his first date with Rachel. They had met at a campus party and he wanted to make a big impression on her.

"My turn," said Jack.

"Let's see some cash," said the thin man. Jack rifled through his wallet and produced two $20 bills. This time the stranger quickly moved the bottle tops. However, Jack was sure that he could win. And he did. Feeling confident he agreed to the stranger's challenge of double or nothing. This round he lost, but he thought he had almost won. So he played double or nothing again. He lost again.

Three bottle tops and a small ball are commonly used in the shell game.

Jack was furious because he suspected the stranger was cheating. But he could not prove it. He was now broke and became very angry, demanding his money back.

At this point, a man who had been sitting nearby drew a revolver and told the thin man to freeze.

"Don't panic," he said. "I'm a plainclothes police officer!" He led the thin man away at the next stop. The bearded man who had originally won $20 also got off at the same stop.

Analysis

The shell game is a very old con game and may take the form of card tricks. Again, three accomplices were involved, the thin man, the man who won the initial $20 and yes, the "police officer."

Jack could never have guessed correctly because the ball was not under any of the bottle tops. His win the first time was a ruse to draw him deeper into the game.

Do not let your ego and false bravado lead you into a no-win situation. You can be sure that if Jack had tried to take back his money, he could have been shot to death by the "police officer."

The best way to win this con is not to play. Realize that people like this rarely work alone. And even if you did win, they would follow you from the train and mug you.

Con men exploit a very human characteristic. The term used to describe this characteristic coined by behavioral scientists is "escalation of commitment." Often to appear consistent, and to save face, we sometimes continue a commitment that we know we should stop. A con artist realizes this and will often use this against you.

In the shell game for example, after Jack had lost $20 he probably sensed something was wrong. Although he could have considered his initial investment a loss, he justified his previous commitment by adding more money.

In the case of the woman and the child, if you had asked Harry if he would let a strange child roam about his apartment unattended, undoubtedly he would have said "no." Yet because he had invited the mother and child into his apartment, he extended his trust to total strangers.

You can protect yourself against cons if you follow these guidelines:

- Do not hand over money to strangers.

- Back out if someone asks you for money that you cannot afford to lose or you become suspicious.

- Be wary of becoming involved just because other people are involved, too, or you will often be suckered by an accomplice.

- Set limits in all situations. If the limit is reached, walk away or at least take a break to regroup your thoughts.

- At every point in the situation, ask yourself truly why you are continuing, and if the answer is counter to solid reasoning, stop and walk away. You must continually remind yourself of the costs involved.

As always, you are responsible for your own safety, so take appropriate safety measures to avoid an escalation to the red state, in which you will have to use defensive tactics.

Chapter 9

Choosing a Self-Defense Course

Self-defense is 70 percent mental preparedness and 30 percent physical skill. All of us practice self-defense in one form or another whenever we avoid a potentially dangerous situation. Should a physical confrontation be unavoidable, knowledge of self-defense techniques will increase your chance of survival. Knowledge of self-defense techniques will also increase your confidence and teach you your physical limitations.

How to Choose a Self-Defense Program

If you are interested in self-defense courses, this section will help you evaluate the many programs available. The teaching of martial arts is not a regulated industry, so anyone can put on a black belt and call himself a martial arts instructor. I recommend training in a short course, then follow up with long-term training. The following sections are guidelines for determining if the training offered fits your self-defense goals. Visit a class, observe the instructor and students, and ask yourself the following questions:

Evaluating an Instructor

- What are the instructor's credentials? Are they verifiable? Since martial arts instruction is not regulated, many instructors make false claims. Call martial arts federations to which the individual claims to belong.

- What would the instructor be doing if he were not teaching seminars? If you think that he is incapable of doing anything else, then do not consider learning from him.

- Can the instructor communicate effectively? Fighting is 70 percent mental preparedness, so if he can only teach you the physical techniques, the instruction is insufficient.

- Does the instructor have an understanding of American culture? If not, the sessions may be unrealistic and the mental preparedness may be inadequate.

- Does the instructor answer questions clearly? If an instructor is reluctant or unable to answer questions, he may be hiding his lack of knowledge or he may be a poor communicator. Questions should be treated with respect.

- Does the instructor offer individualized attention? You should feel that your individual concerns are addressed. Avoid courses in which the student-to-teacher ratio is too large.

- Does the instructor stress continued training? If he promises that you will be able to stop any attacker in two lessons, he is lying. A legitimate instructor will encourage further training.

Evaluating a Self-Defense Seminar

- Are the classes taught from a perspective of everyday situations? If you are learning to defend against unrealistic attacks, you are wasting your time.

- Are the techniques easy to learn? If you cannot learn the mechanics of a technique quickly, the method may be too complicated to use if your life is threatened.

- Are the techniques easy to remember? If you have to memorize them you will probably be unable to use them effectively in a real confrontation. Techniques should work on simple principles that your body can easily remember, even when your mind does not.

- Are the techniques specific to one situation? Every situation will be slightly different, so one technique should be usable in many circumstances.

- Do the techniques require you to warm up before you can perform them? Your assailant will not be likely to give you a half-hour to stretch out before assaulting you.

- Do the techniques require strength, stamina, and excellent physical conditioning? If they do, they are inappropriate. When practicing, always assume the worst case: that your attacker has more strength, stamina, and physical conditioning than you do.

- Is contact against live, moving targets used? If you are practicing striking air, you may not know your own limitations when you actually have to deliver strikes with full power.

- Is verbal abuse used? To create a realistic environment, verbal abuse is sometimes appropriate when attacking.

Evaluating a Martial Arts Program for Long-Term Training

- Are the classes close to home? If not, you may have difficulty attending. To become proficient will require at least two hours a week of long-term training.

- Is sport, mysticism, or knowledge of foreign cultures a heavy emphasis in the classes? The primary emphasis should be realistic, modern self-defense. Anything else is a distraction from this goal.

- Do the techniques increase strength, stamina, and physical conditioning? While these are not necessary for effective self-defense, they increase your odds of survival.

- Does the instructor do most of the teaching or does he delegate it to non-black-belt students? An instructor can often correct technique flaws more quickly than someone who is just learning the techniques. In general, someone should have a minimum of three years of training in the particular art before he is even qualified to be an assistant instructor. He should have five years of training to teach.

• Is the martial art touted as the ultimate martial art? There are no ultimate martial arts. Every art has strengths and weaknesses, but some arts are more suited to different goals. For example, Judo is a grappling sport.

Evaluating Traditional Martial Arts for Self-Defense

Correctly categorizing every martial art is difficult because each martial art has several different styles and some instructors have cross-trained in other martial arts and borrowed techniques. For example, a Karate instructor may have trained in Judo. He may then teach Judo throws to his students while calling them Karate techniques.

The following is a general description of the more popular martial arts.

Karate: This art emphasizes strikes and kicks against vital areas of the body. It contains self-defense, sporting, and meditative elements. Traditionally, much of karate training is done through prearranged fighting patterns called "Kata."

Kung Fu: Kung Fu is a generic term for the martial arts of China. Most forms of kung fu emphasize the "spiritual" and meditative elements, for example, Tai Chi. Generally, styles with this emphasis are unsuitable for modern self-defense without years of training; however, there are some exceptions, such as the kung fu style Wing Chun.

Judo: Judo is an Olympic sport, derived from the combat art ju-jutsu. Judo has techniques that can be used for self-defense, but its primary emphasis is for sport.

Ju-Jutsu: Ju-jutsu, sometimes spelled ju-jitsu, was the unarmed art of the samurai. It is a no-holds-barred self-defense art used by many military and police organizations around the world. I strongly recommend training in ju-jutsu if self-defense is your primary interest.

Tae kwon do: Tae kwon do emphasizes high kicks and strikes. Some of tae kwon do's techniques are suitable for self-defense, but it is an Olympic sport and as such, most of the training is geared toward sport.

Aikido: Aikido is a nonoffensive martial art that emphasizes a harmonizing philosophy. While seeking these higher ideals, most aikido schools disregard effective combat techniques. However, because aikido is a modern derivative of the combat art ju-jutsu, many of its techniques can be modified for self-defense.

Hapkido: Hapkido incorporates the striking techniques of tae kwon do with the combat techniques of ju-jutsu, making it a very effective art for self-defense.

Chapter 10

The Law and Self-Defense

The Bar Fight

"You're sitting in my seat!" yelled the red-faced man from the other side of the bar.

Bill looked at him, surprised. He had just entered the bar a few minutes ago with his friend Stacy. The bar was almost empty and Bill knew that the table he and Stacy had taken was not occupied. Besides, Bill had noticed the man had been sitting at the bar with friends.

"No problem," said Bill. He and Stacy got up and moved to another table. The red-faced man lumbered over, followed by two of his friends.

"Now you're sitting next to my woman," the man said and sat down on the other side of Stacy.

"Why don't you just leave us alone?" Bill asked angrily.

"You college boys think you're so tough. Let's step outside and see how tough you are."

Despite Stacy's protest that they just leave, Bill got up and followed the man outside. He was confident that he would win any fight. He always carried a knife for self-defense and he was not worried.

Outside the man struck Bill. Bill quickly retaliated by drawing the knife and cutting the man across his face. The man yelled in pain and ran off.

Later when Bill was discussing the incident with his roommates, he heard a knock on the door. It was the police and they arrested Bill for aggravated battery.

Analysis

Bill did not fully understand the consequences of his defensive actions. He should have followed Stacy's advice and just left. Instead, he is now about to face the emotional, legal, and financial costs of a rash action. Many students could get into the same situation because they do not know what legally constitutes a threat.

Even though the man was originally taunting Bill, in the eyes of the law, mere words are not enough to constitute a threat. Allow an individual "bragging rights." Let him vent his anger in words. You should never strike first if someone only makes jeering remarks. However, if a man says he is going to shoot you and then reaches into his pocket as though reaching for a gun, you would be justified to strike first.

Define your personal space. Your space should be within one arm's length of your body. If you feel threatened, do not allow someone to get too close to you, which would make defensive actions more difficult. Similarly, in a potential acquaintance rape situation if a person touches you in a threatening manner and you have set limits and told the other person about your set limits, you are justified in using defensive tactics.

Self-Defense and the Law

The law clearly recognizes your right to self-defense. Generally, the law allows you to use reasonable force against an aggressor. If your life is threatened, you can use whatever force is necessary to stop the aggressor. Although the man attacked first, Bill consented to the fight, so whether he gained the right of self-defense is not clear-cut. In this case Bill consented to a battery by accepting the stranger's offer to step outside, much like two boxers agreeing to fight each other. In effect, they have consented to a battery. If the police had come across both men brawling, the two may have been arrested for disorderly conduct. What is clear is that Bill escalated the situation by drawing and using a weapon. Aggravated battery is where a person intentionally uses a weapon to injure another. At this point Bill is guilty of aggravated battery. Assault occurs when a person is physically injured intentionally by another person.

When Bill was arrested, the police officers informed him of his rights. These rights, called Miranda rights, are based on a Supreme Court decision that requires arresting officers to inform apprehended suspects of their rights. The suspects can then waive those rights and give a statement, or remain silent until they have consulted an attorney.

Resisting arrest is against the law, so you can be charged with this crime even if you are innocent of the charges for which you are arrested. If you are arrested, cooperate fully with the police. Police officers typically deal with many difficult individuals in a day. The officer will likely treat you with respect if you offer no resistance. The arresting officer is only performing his sworn duty to uphold law and order. Remember, you are innocent until you have been proven guilty by a court of law.

Miranda Rights

- You have the right to remain silent and are not required to answer any questions.

- Anything you say, can and will be used against you in a court of law.

- You have the right to consult an attorney before you answer any questions and an attorney may be present during the questioning.

- If you have no funds to hire a lawyer, one will be appointed at no cost to you to represent you before and during any questioning if you so desire.

I would recommend always seeking counsel before giving a statement. Bill should secure the best counsel that he can afford. Many campuses have legal aid offices that can help you find attorneys. You run a larger risk of losing your case when you don't use an attorney.

What Right Do I Have to Defend a Friend?

If you come to someone's aid during a fight, you assume their right of self-defense. If you reasonably believe the person you are defending is in imminent danger of bodily harm, you can defend that person with equal or lesser force than the assailant uses. If someone were punching your friend, you would not be justified in stabbing the attacker in the back. Yet you would be justified in using unarmed defensive tactics that were non-life-threatening.

What Do I Do After an Attack?

Never tamper with physical evidence. Suppose in the story the man had drawn the knife and Bill had defended himself by killing the man with a club lying on the street. If Bill then went over and picked up the knife, he would have erased the attacker's fingerprints and replaced them with his own, causing doubt as to whether the man had ever drawn a knife. (The man's friends could lie and say that Bill had planted the knife.) Also realize that any clothing that you wore can be used as physical evidence, so do not wash them or discard them.

Report the incident soon. The law may be more sympathetic to the individual who reports the crime first. The assumption is that you have nothing to hide if you report the crime first. You may want to contact a lawyer. You or your lawyer should give the police the full details of the crime and how you can be reached. When reporting the incident, do not tell the police that you have received any self-defense training. If you are perceived as an expert your martial arts training could be viewed as a deadly weapon.

If You Cannot Walk Away

If you do not think your physical well-being is threatened, walk away. If you think that a threat can lead to violence, also walk away. But sometimes you cannot walk away. If, for example, you are in an elevator and someone is making threatening remarks, reason with the attacker if possible, using direct language. If an attack occurs, react as efficiently as possible. Worry about legal ramifications later. Follow the old saying: **It is far better to be tried by 12 than carried by six!**

Chapter 11

Student Defensive Tactics Short Course

History of this Course

The defensive tactics in this book are derived from a fighting method developed by Antonio Pereira. He combined elements of judo, karate, aikido, classical ju-jutsu, and street fighting into a style he called Miyama Ryu Ju-jutsu. Some of his techniques were later used by one of his students, Dr. John Lewis, who designed a short self-defense course for college students at Northwestern University.

My training in traditional martial arts began as a boy of 12. My personal research in the short course began in 1983, first as a physical training coordinator for a student safety patrol group, and then as assistant instructor of the Northwestern University self-defense course. The student defensive tactics course is based on subsequent years of experience teaching both traditional and short courses at other colleges, as well as to police groups.

How to Use this Course

The course is presented in five lessons. Each lesson builds on the previous ones. The techniques in the course do not require excellent physical conditioning, athletic prowess, strength, or prior martial arts training. The techniques are all easily learned and retained. They are applied according to several simple principles as opposed to specific reactions to specific attacks, enabling you to improvise and make up effective defensive techniques on the spot.

The drills involve full contact with a practice partner so you learn how to concentrate and use your power effectively. The drills also should be practiced with a live partner delivering realistic attacks.

The defensive tactics drills incorporate realistic scenarios and verbal intimidation to teach you to overcome fear and help reduce shock. Students should not neglect this part of the training because even a person with years of training in traditional martial arts may freeze when verbally intimidated.

The techniques can be used against armed or unarmed attackers, without modification. With the use of training weapons in a class, you quickly learn your limitations. This course can be completed in about 12 hours of training. These techniques should only be practiced in the presence of a certified defensive-tactics teacher. To find out seminar information, write to:

Modern Bu-jutsu, Inc.
P.O. Box 703-A
Westmont, IL 60559

Principles of the Student Defensive Tactics System

The Student Defensive Tactics System was developed so that your body can "remember" the techniques even when your mind cannot.

This course will teach you techniques for evasive body positioning, strikes, takedowns, and how to use natural weapons.

The core principle of the system is to apply the techniques to first evade, then strike, and finally, if necessary, take down an attacker. You can escape either after an evasion, a strike, or a takedown. Ideally, you evade an attack, then punish through the use of a strike and a takedown, or a choke and then escape. Only if the attacker is still able to attack do you apply a takedown technique.

By using this principle, you can modify the techniques to fit your needs in any defensive tactics situation.

Another concept you should apply when using this system is "mind before impact." This idea is frequently applied by sports players. For example, a basketball player takes a shot and just as the ball leaves his hands, he visualizes the ball going through the hoop.

While defending yourself, visualize yourself successfully defeating an adversary and escaping the attack. Visualization occurs after an initial evasion and is nearly simultaneous, but slightly before the impact of the strike. As you strike, but before the attacker is hit, imagine not that you are going to strike, but that you have already struck, the attacker is reeling in pain, and you have escaped. By using this visualization, you quicken the speed of your motions and you are even more likely to be successful in defending yourself.

Lesson 1

Attacks

To have a realistic practice session, you must learn to defend from realistic attacks. Other times, you will assume the role of the attacker, so you must learn how to attack properly. Since most students have never attacked anyone, the first lesson teaches you how to identify and carry out various attacks.

Distances of Attacks

Several distances are considered in a physical confrontation. The first distance is an attack that is effective from more than three steps away. This distance usually involves firearms. The best way to defend against an attack at this distance is through street smarts and mental preparedness. An example of defensive tactics at this distance is, if you see a man running toward you firing a gun in your direction, you dive for cover in a nearby building, and then escape out the back door.

The second distance of an attack is from two steps away. The attack involves weapons such as a club, baseball bat, or machete. The vital fact is that now the defender is in effective fighting range; he is now close enough to the attacker so that he can defend himself with defensive tactics. Defenses include meeting the weapon or avoiding it. If you step in to meet the attack, you must do so quickly.

The third distance of an attack is launched from about one step away. The attacker is unarmed or carrying a short weapon, such as a blackjack or knife.

Body-to-body contact defines the fourth distance. Here the attack is effective from less than an arm's length.

Any effective defense system must include preparation for attacks at these four distances. All are equally important. As the defender, you

An attack from more than three steps away is best avoided by street smarts or running away.

must try to control the distance of the attack. On the street if someone you perceive as hostile steps too close to you, either move away or ask them firmly to step back. Even if you make an incorrect assumption, using these tactics is far better than dying from a knife wound because you didn't have time to react fast enough.

Swinging Attack:

This is one of the more common attacks in which fists or bludgeoning weapons are involved. It is usually executed in a swinging manner; the attacker draws back his arm and strikes, using his complete momentum. Target areas are usually the face, the side of the body, or the legs. Examples of a swinging attack are a roundhouse punch, a slap, a slash to the face with a knife, or a club slap to the side of the head.

Practice Drills

Speed of practice: The pace of all drills should be about one-quarter the speed of an actual attack. As you and your partner learn the attacks and defenses, the speed of the attack should be increased in quarter increments.

Roundhouse Punch

• Start without your partner.

• Use verbal intimidation. For example, "I'm going smash your head in!"

• Curl the fingers of your right hand and make a tight fist. Bring your fist slightly behind your head to face height.

• Step forward with your left foot and swing your fist toward an imaginary defender's jaw. Because you do not make contact, you should follow through with your swing.

• Now with a partner, start one step away. Initially, bring your fist as close as possible to the defender's jaw, but do not follow through with the punch. When your partner has learned defensive strategies, follow through with your swing.

Face Slap with a Club

- Start without your partner and hold a training club in your right hand.

- Use verbal intimidation. For example, "I'm going to knock your face in, b___!"

- Bring the training club slightly behind your head to face height.

- Step forward with your right foot and swing your club toward an imaginary defender's jaw. Because you do not make contact, you should follow through with your swing.

- Now with a partner, hold the training club and start about two steps away from him. Initially, bring the club as close as possible to the defender's jaw, but do not follow through with the swing. When your partner has learned defensive strategies, follow through with your swing.

Thrusting Attack:

This attack involves any linear thrusting motions or downward or upward chopping motions. Examples are a push, a thrust to the stomach with a knife, or an overhead club swing to the top of the head. As with the swinging attack, the attacker will try to gain more power in his attack by cocking his attacking arm.

Practice Drills

Stomach Thrust

- Start without your partner.

- Use verbal intimidation. For example, "I'm going to make you bleed."

- Clutch a training knife in your right hand. Step forward with your right foot and stab at an imaginary defender's stomach. Because you do not make contact, you should thrust until your right arm is straightened out.

- Now with a partner, hold the training knife and start one step away from him. Initially, bring the knife as close as possible to his stomach, but do not follow through with the thrust.

- When your partner has learned defensive strategies, follow through with your thrust.

Overhead Stab

- Start without your partner.

- Use verbal intimidation. For example, "You're dead, you son of a b____!"

- Clutch a training knife in your right hand. Bring the knife above shoulder height.

- Step forward with your right foot and stab in a downward arc toward an imaginary defender's throat. Because you do not make contact, you should thrust until your right arm is straightened out.

- Now with a partner, hold the training knife and start one step away from him. Initially, bring the knife as close as possible to his throat, but do not follow through with the stab.

- When your partner has learned defensive strategies, follow through with your thrust.

Grappling Attack:

Many attacks are preceded by grabs. Wrist grabs are very common when an attacker believes that he is stronger than his victim. Frontal grabs are also common when two people are trying to intimidate each other by holding the other in place. Choking also falls into this category. Man's instinct, when unarmed, is to attempt to kill by attacking the neck. Many violent deaths occur when a victim's trachea is blocked, asphyxiating the victim.

In other grappling attacks, called rear body grabs, the adversary grabs you from behind. With body grabs from the rear, attacks are above the elbows, below the elbows, under the arms, and around the neck. You are already in serious trouble for two reasons. First, if the attacker is able to grab you, he probably is able to hit or stab you from behind. Second, he probably has one or more accomplices.

Any of these grappling attacks mean that your initial evasion tactics were unsuccessful and you have immediately moved to a code red.

Practice Drills

Wrist grab

- Start one step away from your partner.

- Use verbal intimidation. For example, "Come here, you little f____!"

- Grab both of her wrists tightly so that your fingers are pointing downward.

- Continue your verbal intimidation while pulling her about the room.

Frontal Grab

- Start one step away from your partner.

- Use verbal intimidation. For example, "I'm going shake the s___ out of you!"

- Grab the front of his clothing tightly.

- Continue your verbal intimidation while shaking the defender or dragging him about the room.

Front Choke

- Start one step away from your partner.

- Use verbal intimidation. For example, "You're dead!"

- Grab her with both hands around her throat, but not too tightly or you may injure your partner.

- Continue your verbal intimidation while pretending to strangle her.

Rear Body Grab over Arms

- Grab your partner from behind, around her chest and both arms. You must leave no space between your front and her back.

- Use verbal intimidation. For example, "You're coming with me b____!"

- Hold her in place or pick her up and carry her if you can. Continue your verbal intimidation.

Rear Body Grab under Arms

- Grab your partner from behind, around her chest and under her arms. You must leave no space between your front and her back.

- Use verbal intimidation. For example, "Do as I say, and you won't be hurt!"

Rear Choke

• Grab your partner from behind, with your right arm around her neck. You must leave no space between your front and her back.

• Use verbal intimidation. For example, "Just give me what I want!"

Ground Attack

In this attack the victim has fallen or has been thrown to the ground. Attacks include rape, specific pins, chokes, and punches while on the ground.

Practice Drills

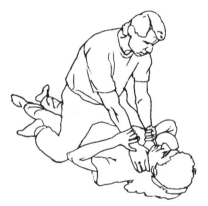

Double-Hand Choke

• Sit on the defender's stomach as she lies on her back.

• Reach over and choke her with both hands, but not too tightly.

• Use verbal intimidation. For example, "Just hold still and you'll enjoy this."

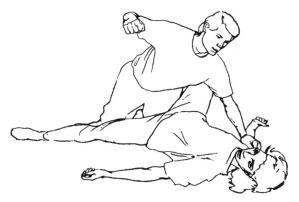

Roundhouse Punch

- Kneel between the defender's legs as she lies on her back. Hold her by the shoulder with your left hand.

- Use verbal intimidation. For example, "I'm going to kill you!"

- Curl the fingers of your right hand and make a tight fist. Bring your right fist slightly behind your head to face height.

- Swing your right fist slowly toward the defender's jaw.

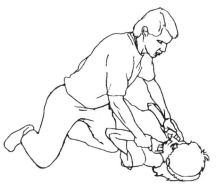

Pinning Both Arms

- Kneel on the defender's right side as she lies on her back.

- Grab both of her wrists and pin them in front of her chest.

- Use verbal intimidation. For example, "Lie still, you c___ or I'll kill you!"

Hints for Practicing in Class

Put your ego and pride aside and do not be afraid to make mistakes because the time to make them is in the presence of your instructor. During my years of training I have, and will continue to, make many mistakes in the classroom so that I can know my limitations if I am attacked.

Some students learn a couple of "tricks" and think they are experts. Knowledge of single techniques specific to a few situations is not enough. Continued practice is necessary to master an integrated system of defense, as well as timing and dynamics.

You are responsible for your safety and the safety of your training partner. Enthusiasm is good, but the pain from injury is real. Be careful of working with someone who is too rambunctious. If your partner does not practice with safety in mind, get another partner. During class time, injury is your only real enemy.

Practice involves teamwork. When first learning the drills, the defender should be given a chance to position himself for a fall, particularly if he lacks experience. And the attacker should not resist when the defender responds with a defensive technique. Some may argue, "Nobody is going to stand there and let you apply all those techniques." True, but students must begin by practicing slowly so they can master the techniques.

Later, during rapid-order drills in which both attacker and defender are well-versed, attacks must be accurate and at full speed and power. Mock weapons should be used, such as padded clubs and wooden knives. Treat them as real; although your training knife is made of wood, do not treat it as a stick. For obvious reasons do not work with real knives.

When you are the attacker, your role is to prepare the defender, mentally and physically, to survive an actual street attack. The attacker must maintain control to avoid injuries, but he must forget himself for the moment and become an intimidating adversary. Without an aggressive attacker, defenses will quickly lose their flavor.

I have had the displeasure of witnessing several martial arts demonstrations in which the attacker execute an attack without true injurious intent. While the defender usually reacted with plausible techniques, the exercise is not realistic. If the adversary does not attack with intent in class, he is doing the defender a grave disservice. The defender now believes that he possesses some skill. Unfortunately, that skill is untested. This rule of intent applies even when you are first learning a technique.

After the defender has begun his counterattack, an attacker must learn to react. If a counterpunch is aimed at the attacker's head, he should simulate being struck.

When you are the defender, you should imagine that the attack is real. Imagine that you are afraid or angry. (A range of emotions are experienced during an attack that are difficult to duplicate in class.) Anticipate an adversary's counters. Take into account the intelligence of the attacker. Consider whether he will attempt to draw his weapon after his initial attack. If, however, you treat the training as a sport or physical exercise, the techniques will not work in real life. Training has numerous health benefits, but you should practice these techniques primarily for their self-protection value. Never forget the seriousness behind an attack.

Learning to remain calm is perhaps the most important aspect of practice, and the most difficult concept to grasp. Control of your emotions is necessary to avoid anticipating an attack, and to effectively assess your entire surroundings. To react efficiently you must react quickly, then become calm between your counterattacks. Uncontrolled emotion leads to tunnel vision, causing you to concentrate on only one attacker and ignore the others. Skilled fighters sometimes lose in street confrontations because of tunnel vision.

Students often are discouraged because a technique works in class, but does not seem to work when applied on a friend. The techniques are more than just a series of movements. The mind-set behind the action is as important. The techniques are not designed for play or to be done casually. If you are not prepared to hurt this friend, do not try the techniques. As a general rule, do not train with people who are not practitioners. You have nothing to prove; all the techniques have been refined in actual combat.

Lesson 2

Evasive Body Positions

The best way to avoid an attack is to move your body out of the way. This principle applies in all of the states of awareness of the color code. When an untrained person is attacked, his first reaction is usually to attempt to block the attack with his hands or to jump completely out of the way of the attack.

The problem with these responses is if you are attacked by an armed adversary, a direct block may likely be collapsed. Or if you avoid the attack completely and you are unable to escape, the adversary may attack again, this time a little wiser because of your earlier deception.

Our goal is to first move the body out of the way of the attack and leave the defender in a position to retaliate if necessary. This retaliation will depend on your environment and each individual situation. For example, if you are attacked in an elevator, you will probably be able to avoid an attack only for a short time.

For your initial evasion to be effective, you must take into account natural tendencies. For example, if you were startled by the attack, your natural reaction probably would be to move backward. But if you had anticipated the attack and were angry, your natural tendency might be to move forward.

In your initial evasion, both circular and linear motions must be used. Our goal is to use an ancient martial arts principle called "ju" or pliancy. When you are pushed, you should pull and when pulled, push. By acting counter to your adversary's expectations, you add your physical strength to his and defeat him through the use of his own momentum. Sounds esoteric, doesn't it? Actually, most combative martial arts are based on scientific principles. And the effectiveness of the techniques should not surprise anybody because the samurai warriors lived and died by their martial techniques. Techniques that did not work did not survive their creators.

Without a thorough knowledge of initial evasion techniques, further training is pointless because if you cannot avoid an attack, offensive capabilities will be irrelevant.

Hints for Practicing Body Positions

These steps are simple and easy to remember. Practice these steps at home as a dance, always coming back to a natural position in between defenses. When you practice, try to feel the emotions you would experience if you were attacked. Pretend that you are afraid as you step back, or pretend that you are angry as you step forward. Look at your adversary at all times. Concentrate, and fight the instinct to turn away and run.

Practice these body positions imagining attacks from different angles. For example, from a sitting or lying position, your hip movement will be restricted, but twisting your shoulders and hips will still allow you to avoid an attack.

Stances

The two combatants circle each other. Sweat drips off their bodies as they glare at each other. Finally, one raises his right knee and spreads his arms. The other assumes a catlike stance. They begin to emit animal sounds in preparation for a strike.

These stances are what most people, including many martial artists, picture as fighting stances. As a college student interested in self-defense, you must make your everyday stance your fighting stance. Any defensive tactics must become natural. If you have to think, "I must now assume a defensive posture," your response may already be too late if you are suddenly attacked. Besides, of what use are these esoteric fighting postures if you are attacked suddenly in a car or small room? Your everyday stance is the best fighting stance because it gives nothing away. If you clench your fist and drop into a martial arts pose, you have lost any possible element of surprise. Although indicating that you are prepared to fight may be an effective deterrent in a date rape situation, such a strategy on the street can cause problems.

First of all, you should not treat fighting as a sport. Until a committed attack is launched at you, you should be using your street smarts to avoid a fight. Fighting is a last resort, and you may aggravate the situation by revealing your hand too soon. If the adversary believes that you are a competent defender, but he is still committed to the attack, he may now attack more cautiously, and thus make defense more difficult for you. Finally, by taking a martial arts stance, you have indicated that you are prepared to fight and some witnesses may view you as an aggressor.

Natural Position

The natural position is the superior fighting stance. Stand with your back straight and head up. Your feet should be about shoulders' width apart. Hands should hang loosely at your sides. Your balance should be slightly forward, as if you are leaning into the situation. Your weight should only be distributed about 60 percent toward the balls of your feet. If you shift more than 60 percent of your weight forward, your heels will leave the ground and make the stance unnatural. Your knees should be bent slightly and not locked.

The natural position

The "chill out" position

The natural position has several variations. For example, placing one leg forward and pivoting your hips 45 degrees affords you some protection from a sudden attack. Another variation is the natural position while seated. The same principle of leaning slightly forward applies. You should be prepared to defend from any of the attacks while seated. A third variation is the "chill out" position, so-called because you bring your hands up automatically as you try to defuse the situation verbally. Place one leg forward and pivot your hips 45 degrees to protect you from a surprise attack. Bring both hands up, palms facing outward. As you do so, try to verbally de-escalate the situation. All of these natural positions are nonoffensive gestures.

The natural position is the most relaxed one a human can assume while still remaining attentive. Professional public speakers as well as negotiators who want to appear extremely attentive often use this position. The stance is very natural, requires no additional training, and indicates alertness, yet is nonaggressive. If you lean backward, you may seem off balanced and too relaxed. An assailant may infer from this body language that you would be too slow to respond to his attack.

Here's an example to illustrate how body language works in a minor argument. If you are arguing with somebody who is fidgeting, rocking from side to side, and not looking directly at you, you assume that he is very uncomfortable and he may be avoiding eye contact because he is lying or trying to hide something. You probably think you can win the dispute if your arguments are of equal merit. However, if somebody is looking you directly in the eye, leaning into the situation, and arguing point for point, you probably do not feel as confident.

Similarly, an attacker will "read" his potential victim's body language. If a criminal has a choice between victimizing someone who looks as if he is easy prey or someone who looks as if he is going to put up a fight, the attacker will choose the easy prey. Even predatory animals go after the weaklings in a herd.

Ground Defensive Position

During a football game, if an injured player is lying on his back with feet outstretched, fans assume the injury is serious. If, however, they see the same player with one knee up, even if he is flat on his back, they may assume that he was just dazed or else he wouldn't have had the presence of mind to put up at least one knee. This same principle can be applied to self-defense. If you are thrown to the ground, the first rule of thumb is to never lie flat; keep at least one knee up. Not only will this move indicate your preparedness to fight, but it is an automatic protection against someone trying to stamp a male victim's groin.

When on the ground, you want to keep the attacker from sitting on your stomach. If he sits on your stomach, he will severely limit your mobility and you may not be able to move your legs and hips to provide power in your escapes. While you are on the ground, you want to regain your footing as soon as possible and still use some basic body positioning.

Ground defensive position

The adversary can attack from several directions, but he usually will attack from the side or from the front because he wants to control you. The ideal defensive position involves placing one knee between you and your adversary. To get your knee up from the side you may need to bring your heel to your buttocks and twist from one shoulder to the other. When you twist, make sure that you do not keep your back flat on the ground. If you do, your mobility is severely limited. When the adversary attacks, lodge the knee closest to him to separate you from him.

Body Position 1

This evasion is useful against any nonswinging, standing attack. When moving your body out of danger, think of a graph with an xy-plane. If we assume that you are standing in a natural position with your shoulders and hips square to the adversary, your hips are on the x axis. Your feet should be about shoulders' width apart. If they are too far apart, your mobility is restricted. If they are too close together, you can be toppled easily. Your feet should point directly forward.

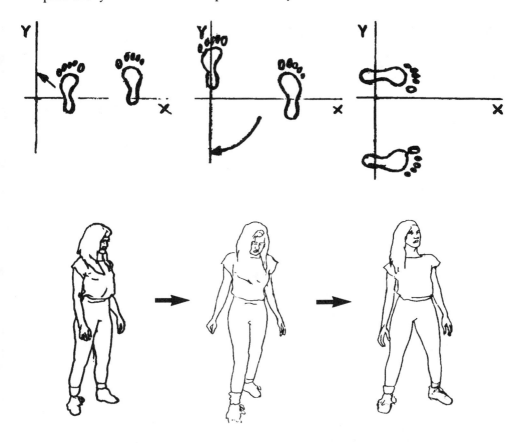

- Take one step forward with your left foot. Twist your hips 90 degrees, clockwise.

- Pivot on your left foot and slide your right foot back so that both feet are again parallel, but on the y axis.

Practice Drills

Scenario:

The attacker attempts to stab you in your stomach with a knife.

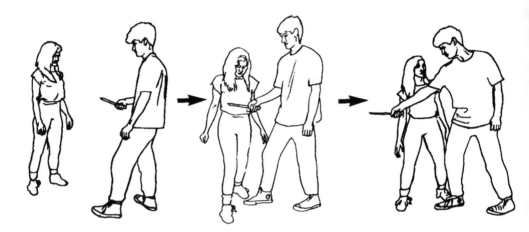

Attacker:

• Start one step away from your partner.
• Use verbal intimidation. For example, "I'm going to cut you."
• Clutch the training knife in your right hand.
• Step forward with your right foot and stab toward the defender's stomach.

Defender:

• Take one small step forward with your left foot. Even though you may seem to be stepping into the attack, you are actually safer than stepping away because the attacker has already begun the attack. You are now in a position to launch a counterattack.
• Twist your hips 90 degrees, clockwise. Pivot on your left foot and slide your right foot back so that both feet are again parallel, but on the y axis.

Scenario:

The attacker attempts to stab you in your throat with a knife.

Attacker:

- Start one step away from your partner.
- Use verbal intimidation. For example, "You're dead, you son of a b____!"
- Clutch the training knife in your right hand.
- Bring the knife above your shoulder to face height.
- Step forward with your right foot and stab in an arc toward the defender's throat.

Defender:

- Take one small step forward with your left foot. Even though you may seem to be stepping into the attack, you are actually safer than stepping away because the attacker has already begun the attack. You are now in a position to launch a counterattack.
- Twist your hips 90 degrees, clockwise.
- Pivot on your left foot and slide your right foot back so that both feet are again parallel, but on the y axis.

Body Position 2

This evasion is used against a swinging attack such as a roundhouse punch.

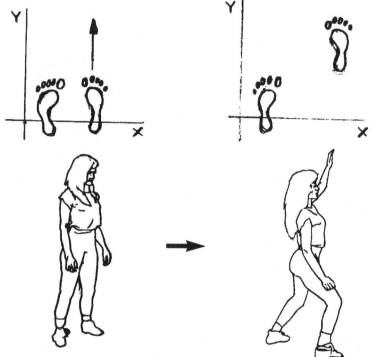

- Start from the natural position, with your hands hanging loosely at your sides.
- Step forward with your right foot. Your right knee should be bent deeply.
- With your palms facing toward your body, bring your right hand across your body until it is in front of your left thigh. Bring your left hand up to the height of your right shoulder, and rotate your palm so it faces outward.
- Swing your left arm, with the palm facing outward, until your arm is the distance of about two fists from your right side. As you swing your left arm away from your body, swing your hips to the left (counterclockwise), causing you to use the power of your whole body. As you execute the block, flex your knees slightly and push off from the ground. Tuck your thumb in and extend your fingers toward the ceiling to make your hand stronger.

Practice Drills

Scenario:

The attacker attempts to hit you using a roundhouse punch.

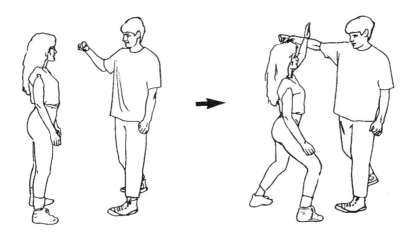

Attacker:

- Start one step away from your partner.
- Use verbal intimidation. For example, "I'm going to punch your face in, b____!"
- Curl the fingers of your right hand and make a tight fist. Bring your fist slightly behind your head to face height.
- Step forward with your left foot and swing your fist toward the defender's jaw.

Defender:

- Start from the natural position, with your hands hanging loosely at your sides.
- As the attacker draws back his fist, step forward with your right foot. Your right knee should be bent deeply.
- Continue steps for Body Position 2. Your left arm should end up about the distance of two fists from your right side.
- As you execute the block, flex your knees slightly and push off from the ground.

Scenario:

The attacker attempts to hit you with a club to the side of your head.

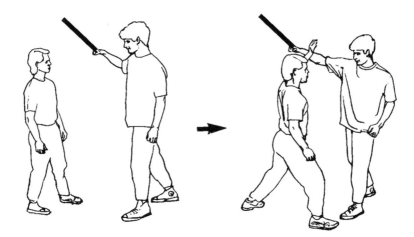

Attacker:

- Start about two steps away from your partner.
- Use verbal intimidation. For example, "I'm going to beat you into the ground!"
- Hold a training club in your hand and bring it slightly behind your head to face height.
- Step forward with your left foot and swing your club toward the defender's jaw.

Defender:

- Start from the natural position, with your hands hanging loosely at your sides.
- As the attacker draws back his fist, step forward with your right foot. Your right knee should be bent deeply.
- Continue steps for Body Position 2. Your left arm should end up about the distance of two fists from your right side.
- As you execute the block, flex your knees slightly and push off from the ground.

Body Position 3

This evasion is useful against any swinging attack.

- Start from the natural position, with your hands hanging loosely at your sides.
- Step slightly to the left with your left foot, bending your knees deeply. Lower your hips, keeping your back straight.
- Raise both hands, positioning them about one fist's length away from your face while bending your elbows. This hand position will enable you to quickly block any follow-up attack.

Practice Drills

Scenario:

The attacker attempts to punch you.

Attacker:

- Start one step away from your partner.
- Use verbal intimidation. For example, "Take this a__hole!"
- Bring your right fist slightly behind your head to face height. Step forward with your left foot and swing your fist toward the defender's jaw.

Defender:

- Start from the natural position, with your hands hanging loosely at your sides.
- As the attacker slaps, step slightly to the left with your left foot, bending your knees deeply. Lower your hips, keeping your back straight. The fist passes harmlessly over your head.
- Raise both hands, positioning them about one fist's length away from your face while bending your elbows. This hand position will enable you to quickly block any follow-up attack.

Scenario:

The attacker swings toward your face with a club.

Attacker:

- Start one step away from your partner and hold a training club.
- Use verbal intimidation. For example, "I'm going to knock your block off!"
- Hold the training club in your right hand and bring it slightly behind your head to face height.
- Step forward with your right foot and swing the club toward the defender's throat.

Defender:

- Start from the natural position, with your hands hanging loosely at your sides.
- As the attacker swings the club, step slightly to the left with your left foot, bending your knees deeply. Lower your hips, keeping your back straight. The club passes harmlessly over your head.
- Raise both hands, positioning them about one fist's length away from your face while bending your elbows. This hand position will enable you to quickly block any follow-up attack.

Lesson 3

Strikes

Morally, legally, and technically an adversary gives you the advantage if he initiates the attack. The reason you gain a technical edge is that if the adversary attacks first, he must leave some opening for a counterattack. To counterattack, striking and kicking techniques are effective tools.

The first thing that you should do after an evasion of an attack is strike. This strike "unbalances" the adversary, or places him off-guard physically and mentally. You could unbalance him physically by executing a penetrating punch or an aggressive pull, or by throwing a cup of coffee in his face.

These techniques should be accompanied by a loud, bloodcurdling shout. Tighten your abdomen as you shout (to harden your body). The psychological impact of the yell, compounded by the physical pain from the applied technique, will put the adversary on the defensive. The shout will also frighten accomplices.

Police officers often use a similar concept to put a resisting suspect on the defensive. If they apply a technique and the subject is in so much pain he does not know where to go, he may inadvertently hurt himself. So as the technique is applied the officer may say something such as, "Lie face down."

Escape is your primary consideration. So after you block or avoid the attack, and then strike the assailant, you need not stay to finish the fight. The adversary possibly, but not probably, could be defeated solely through striking and kicking. Multiple strikes definitely are not efficient when dealing with multiple attackers. Do not try to turn the fight into a sparring or wrestling match. Never assume that you will defeat your adversary with one blow, even though you must strike as though each blow is the only one that matters.

Strikes should be practiced from three basic positions: standing, sitting, and lying on your back. In all cases you must use the ground and the rotation of your hips and shoulders to generate power. Most of the strikes covered can be executed with a gloved hand, so they are independent of climate.

Where you strike is as important as how you strike. Knowledge of the body's vital areas is essential to successful self-defense, but you must use great care and control. Like all of the techniques presented, knowledge of vital areas was developed through actual feudal combat. For example, during battle the samurai wore light, flexible armor. To strike at random against a sword-wielding adversary meant certain death.

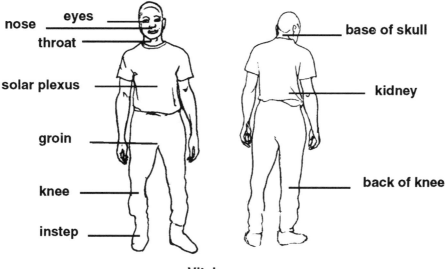

Vital areas

A modern scientific understanding of vital areas also enables you to attack the weakest points of the body. For example, the skull has many sutures, where the bones knit together. To strike at points along these sutures would cause tremendous damage.

Where you strike will depend on the adversary's clothing, the weather, or the nature of the encounter. Today, nobody wears armor. Or do they? The heavy parkas worn by Midwesterners during harsh winters can probably deflect the force of a well-placed blow. Striking the body with precision is difficult if you can't identify vital points through heavy clothing. Similarly, environmental conditions such as a dark alley may make a strike difficult.

Palm Heel Strike

Extend your fingers and push your palm out. Bend your thumb and tuck it against your hand. The striking surface is the palm.

Vital Areas:

Nose, chin, ear, solar plexus, and groin.

Impact Drill

Holder:

- Hold a hand pad at about face height. Tilt the pad forward slightly.
- Put your other hand about six inches behind the pad so that if your partner strikes through, this hand will stop the pad from hitting you in the face.
- The hand holding the pad should not be too rigid as you are simulating a human face, which will move when it is hit.

Defender:

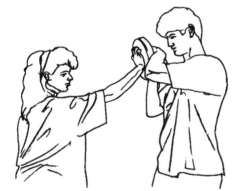

- Visualize striking an adversary's jaw. Practice stepping in, executing each of the three evasive body positions, and striking.
- Exhale loudly and yell "No!" as you strike. Penetrate six inches through the target.

Scenario:

The attacker attempts to slap your face.

Attacker:

- Start one step away from your partner.
- Use verbal intimidation. For example, "Do what I say b____!'"
- Bring your open right hand slightly behind your head to face height. Step forward with your left foot and swing your hand toward the defender's cheek.
- Move your head back to simulate being struck as the defender strikes.

Defender:

- As the attacker draws back his hand, visualize striking the attacker in his jaw.
- Step in with your right foot and block his slap with your left hand (Body Position 2).
- Immediately twist your hips to the left (counter clockwise) and strike his chin with the palm heel.
- Exhale and yell "No!" as you strike.

Knife-Hand Strike

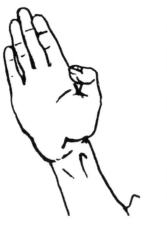

Open your hand. Extend your fingers, pressing them together. Bend your thumb and tuck it against your hand. The striking surface is the "knife edge" of the hand.

Vital Areas:

Nose, throat, collarbone, abdomen, ribs, spleen, and groin.

Impact Drill

Holder:

- Use a hand pad and men should wear a groin cup.
- Step behind the defender and face her right side.
- Hold the pad directly behind her at about groin height.

Defender:

- With the holder behind you, turn your head only and look at the pad.
- Visualize striking an adversary in the groin and him bending over in pain.
- Swing your hand behind you in a downward arc. Strike with the knife edge of your hand and yell "No!" as you strike. Follow through at least six inches behind the pad.

Scenario:

The attacker grabs you from the rear over both arms.

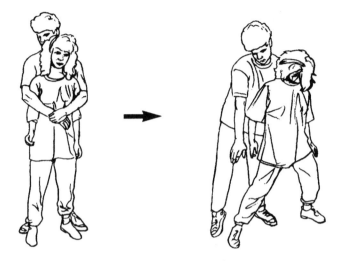

Attacker:

- Grab your partner from behind, around her chest and over both arms. You must leave no space between your front and her back.
- Use verbal intimidation. For example, "If you don't resist, you won't be hurt!"
- Hold her in place or pick her up and carry her if you can. Continue your verbal intimidation. When the defender has struck, simulate being hit in the groin and release the defender.

Defender:

- Step to the side with your left foot, moving your hips to the left of his groin.
- Look at his groin area, visualize him being struck and then strike him with the knife-hand. Exhale and yell "No!" as you strike. (In practice you would slap his thigh to simulate this strike.)

Web strike:

Extend your thumb as far as you can from your index finger. Bend your thumb and fingers in at the first knuckle. Hold the fingers together. Strike with the web of your hand between the index finger and the thumb.

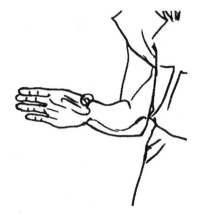

Vital Area:

Throat.

Impact Drill

Holder:

- Tightly roll up a newspaper and hold it at one end about one foot away from your throat. The newspaper should point upward.
- Put your other hand about six inches behind the newspaper so that if your partner strikes through the newspaper, this hand will stop the newspaper from hitting you in the face.
- Do not hold the hand grasping the newspaper too rigidly as you are simulating a human throat, which will move when it is hit.

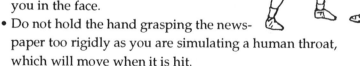

Defender:

- Practice stepping in, executing each of the three evasive body positions and striking.
- Visualize striking an adversary's throat and him reeling from the strike.
- Exhale loudly and yell "No!" as you strike the newspaper.
- Penetrate six inches through the target.

Scenario:

The attacker grabs both of your wrists.

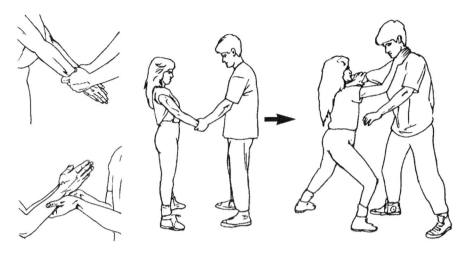

Attacker:

- Start one step away from your partner.
- Use verbal intimidation. For example, "Come here, you little f——!"
- Grab both of the defender's wrists tightly so that your fingers are pointing downward.
- Continue your verbal intimidation while pulling her about the room.
- When she strikes, react as if you've been struck in the throat.

Defender:

- Step forward and force your hands down toward the ground so that the fingertips of both of your hands are touching.
- Keep moving forward and, bending your elbows inward, rotate and bring the hands up as though you were raising your hands in prayer. This move provides escape from the wrist grab by using the thumb side and the bone of your forearm (ulna) against the natural opening of the attacker's forefinger and thumb.
- Visualize striking the adversary's throat and him reeling from the strike. Exhale loudly and yell "No!" as you strike his throat with the web strike.

Elbow Strike:

Strike with the area just above the point of the elbow.

Vital Areas:

Jaw, temple, and rib cage.

Impact Drill

Holder:

- Hold a large striking pad horizontally and flat against your chest.
- Stand directly behind the defender.
- Exhale on impact so that you do not have the wind knocked out of you.

Defender:

- Visualize striking the adversary in his solar plexus and him releasing you.
- Extend your right hand forward so that your arm is parallel to the ground. Make a tight fist and pull the hand back quickly.
- Exhale and yell "No!" as you strike the pad with your elbow. Try to penetrate six inches behind the pad.

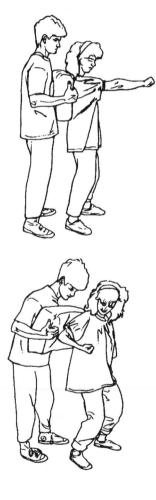

Scenario:

The attacker grabs you from behind around your neck.

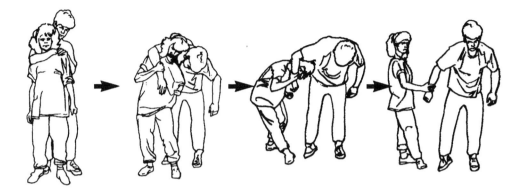

Attacker:

- Grab your partner from behind, with your right arm around her neck. There should be no space between your front and her back.
- Use verbal intimidation. For example, "Come with me baby. You'll like this."
- Walk her backward as if you were taking her to a car.
- Continue your verbal intimidation.
- When you are struck, exhale and release the defender.

Defender:

- When you are grabbed from behind, turn your head into the crook of his right elbow to gain some room to breathe.
- Visualize striking the adversary in his solar plexus and him releasing you.
- Extend your left hand forward so that your arm is parallel to the ground. Make a tight fist and pull the hand back quickly.
- Exhale and yell "No!" as you strike the adversary with your elbow.
- Pull his right hand down, and escape by bringing your head underneath the adversary's right armpit while pivoting on your right foot.

Foot Stomp:

Turn your heel outward and bend the foot upward. Strike with the bottom of your foot.

Vital Areas:

Nose, chin, solar plexus, knee, and instep.

Impact Drill

Holder:

- Kneel on your left knee. Hold a full-length pad against your chest and lean toward the front of the defender, who should lie on her left side.
- Exhale as the defender strikes the pad to avoid having the wind knocked out of you.

Defender:

- Lie on your left side, propped up by your left elbow.
- Visualize striking an attacker in the jaw with the bottom of your foot and causing him to reel back.
- Bring your right knee to your chest. Stomp toward the pad, penetrating at least six inches.
- Exhale as you strike and yell "No!"
- Immediately spring to your feet and escape.

Scenario:

The adversary attempts to punch you on the ground.

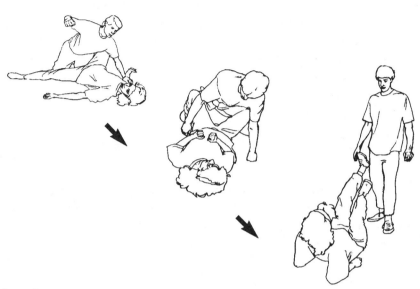

Attacker:

- Kneel between the defender's legs as she lies on her back. Raise your hand to strike her face.
- Use verbal intimidation. For example, "Lie still, you c____, this won't hurt a bit!"

Defender:

- Turn onto your right side, twisting your hips to the right side. Slide your right knee into his stomach (Ground Defensive Position).
- Visualize striking an attacker in the jaw with the bottom of your foot and causing him to reel back.
- Bring your left knee to your chest and stomp toward the adversary's cheek.
- As soon as he is struck, get up and escape.

Lesson 4

Takedowns and Chokes

Takedowns are important to your defensive repertoire because they allow you to stun the aggressor completely so you can escape. Takedowns are devastating physically and mentally to an attacker. When an attacker is suddenly thrown to the ground or into a wall, his perspective suddenly changes. First of all, he is surprised because he has not hit his target. Second, he is discomforted at having the tables turned because he believed he had the upper hand. And most importantly, a takedown shocks the whole body.

Circle Throw

The circle throw takes advantage of an adversary's momentum, allowing you to direct him into an object or to the ground. This momentum is either created from his attack or by an unbalancing strike from you. The circle throw is very versatile and can be used on an individual regardless of his or your physical strength. The circle throw can also be used in confined areas, such as an elevator or a bedroom.

In general, the throw involves controlling the adversary's head with at least one hand, and then using a circle step and the other hand to control his body. You can execute this throw while sitting or standing. You must turn your hips 180 degrees or as much as possible when in a confined area.

Practice Drill:

Scenario:

The attacker attempts to hit you with a roundhouse punch.

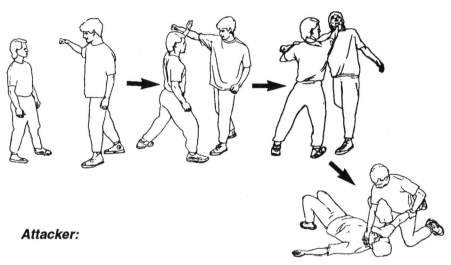

Attacker:

- Start one step away from your partner.
- Use verbal intimidation. For example, "You motherf———, I'm going to knock your head in!"
- Bring your right fist slightly behind your head to face height. Step forward with your left foot and swing your fist toward the defender's jaw. When you are twisted to the ground, fall down on your back and exhale as you hit the ground.

Defender:

- Visualize the adversary lying in a crumpled heap on the ground. Step in with your right foot and block the oncoming punch with your left hand (Body Position 2).
- Yell "No!" loudly as you use the web of your right hand to strike the adversary's throat.
- Grab his throat with your right hand and his right wrist with your left hand. Pivot counterclockwise on your right foot 180 degrees and kneel on your left knee. The adversary will be thrown to the ground.

Scenario:

The adversary attempts a bear hug.

Attacker:

- Start one step away from your partner.
- Use verbal intimidation. For example, "Come here, you little b___!"
- Rush the defender and grab her around her chest and arms.
- When you are twisted to the ground, fall on your back and exhale as you hit the ground.

Defender:

- Visualize the attacker in extreme pain on the ground in front of you.
- Step in with your right foot. Yell "No!" loudly as you strike with the web of your right hand to the adversary's throat.
- Grab his throat with your right hand and his right elbow with your left hand. Pivot counterclockwise on your right foot 180 degrees and kneel on your left knee. The adversary will be thrown to the ground.

Scenario:

The adversary attempts to punch you while your back is to the wall.

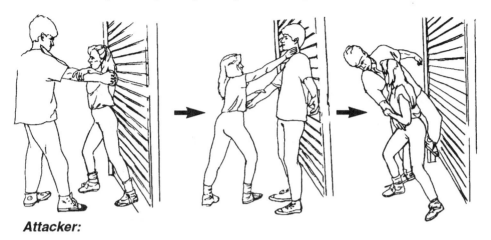

Attacker:

- Start one step away from your partner, whose back is to a wall.
- Use verbal intimidation. For example, "You want to play, lets play!"
- Bring your right fist slightly behind your head to face height. Step forward with your right foot and swing your fist toward the defender's jaw. Your head will be driven toward the wall, so make sure you look at your belt to protect your head from hitting the wall. When you are twisted to the ground, fall on your back and exhale as you hit the ground.

Defender:

- Stand with your back to the wall. Visualize the adversary lying in extreme pain on the ground.
- Step in with your right foot and block the oncoming punch with your left hand. Yell "No!" loudly as you strike with the web of your right hand to the adversary's throat.
- Grab his throat with your right hand and his right wrist with your left hand. Pivot counterclockwise on your right foot 180 degrees and throw the attacker into the wall. His head and body will hit the wall. Maintaining your grip on the adversary's neck, pivot counterclockwise 180 degrees again. The adversary will be thrown to the ground and your back will be against the wall again.

Scenario:

The adversary attempts to push you to the floor of a car.

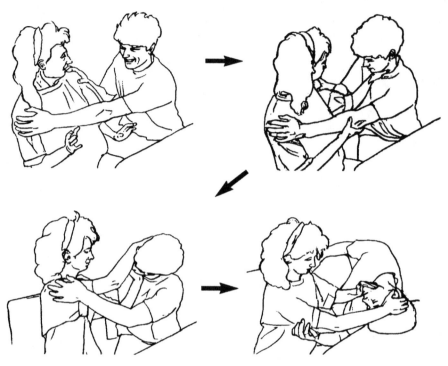

Attacker:

- Reach over and grab the defender's shoulders in an attempt to push her on her back.
- Use verbal intimidation. For example, "You know you want it baby!"

Defender:

- Visualize the attacker reeling backward stunned, and see yourself escaping from the car. Reach up and hit the attacker's throat with a web strike.
- Exhale and yell "No!" as you strike. Grab the top of the attacker's head with your right hand. Grab his chin with your left. Twist his head clockwise and smash it into the car's dashboard. Exit the car immediately and escape.

Scenario:

The adversary attempts to choke you on the ground.

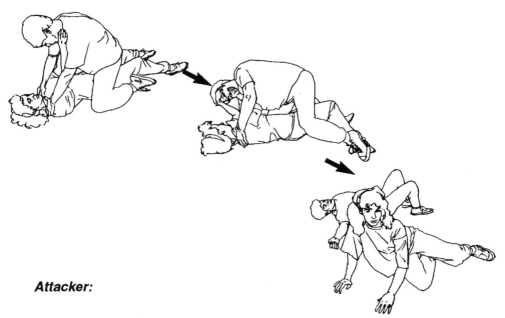

Attacker:

- Sit on the defender's stomach as she lies on her back.
- Reach over and choke her with both hands, but not too tightly.
- Use verbal intimidation. For example, "Just hold still and I won't hurt you."
- When you are twisted to the ground, fall on your back and exhale as you hit the ground.

Defender:

- Visualize the attacker lying on the ground clutching his throat. Reach up and strike the attacker in his throat with a web strike.
- Exhale and yell "No!" as you strike.
- Grab the top of the attacker's head with your left hand. Grab his chin with your right. Twist his head counterclockwise. Turn your hips and shoulders counterclockwise to assist your neck twist.
- When the adversary has been thrown off, get up and escape.

Choking

If an unskilled individual hears that someone was rendered unconscious by choking, he imagines an attacker forcefully crushing a victim's throat. This method of choking is actually inefficient, as it relies on brute strength. This kind of choke is unacceptable for self-defense as the effects of such a choke are too often permanent. The assailant's trachea would probably be crushed, which could cause death.

Our self-defense method of choking is much more efficient. Choking renders an adversary unconscious approximately 10 seconds after the technique is applied and can be applied on any individual, regardless of strength, size, or physical prowess. This powerful tool can be taught very quickly and students tend to retain it for a very long time because of its simplicity.

Pressure can be applied to the side of the neck and/or to the larynx and trachea. If pressure is applied to the larynx or trachea, excruciating pain occurs before unconsciousness. When an adversary has been rendered unconscious, be sure to let him go because squeezing the carotid artery cuts off oxygen to the brain. The individual's face will flush because of the disturbance of the pressure in the carotid arteries and the jugular veins. Then he may suffer convulsions, similar to an epileptic fit. These convulsions occur as the sympathetic nervous system causes an increased heart rate, increased blood pressure, and dilation of the pupils.

An adversary will regain consciousness without assistance within 10-20 seconds, with no permanent injuries. Choking is therefore a humane way to subdue an adversary and gives the student time to escape with minimum injury.

Practice Drill:

Receiver:

- Sit on your heels with your back to the defender.
- As soon as you feel pressure from the choke, slap your body, the ground, or the defender's body signaling to the defender that the choke was effective.

Defender:

- Move in behind the receiver.
- Curl your right arm around the front of his neck. Control his head by placing the back of your right hand against his left cheek. This will also pull the receiver off balance. Place the back of your left hand on the receiver's left shoulder. Bend your left wrist so that your forearm is against the receiver's back. The wrist and forearm should form an L-shape.
- Place your left palm in your right palm. Your right wrist should come in contact with the receiver's throat. Pull your right arm toward you and squeeze the receiver's neck.
- Release as soon as he slaps his body, the ground, or your body.

Scenario:

The adversary attempts to hit your face with a club.

Attacker:

- Start one step away from your partner.
- Use verbal intimidation. For example, "You're mine now, b___!"
- Hold a training club in your right hand and bring it slightly behind your head to face height. Step forward with your right foot and swing the club toward the defender's jaw.
- When you feel pressure from the choke, slap your body, the ground, or the defender's body immediately so the defender knows to release you.

Defender:

- Step forward slightly with your left foot and duck under the arcing club (Body Position 3).
- Visualize the attacker passing out. Step behind the attacker with your right foot. Curl your right arm around the front of his neck. Control his head by placing the back of your right hand against his left cheek.
- Place the back of your left hand on the attacker's left shoulder. Bend your left wrist so that your forearm is against the attacker's back. The wrist and forearm should form an L-shape. Place your right palm in your left palm.
- Your right wrist should come in contact with the attacker's throat. Pull your right arm toward you and squeeze the attacker's neck. Release as soon as he slaps the side of his body, the ground, or your body.

Scenario:

The adversary attempts to slap your face.

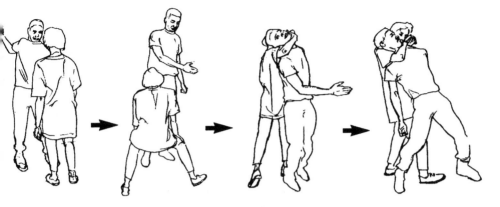

Attacker:

- Start one step away from your partner.
- Use verbal intimidation. For example, "I'm going to slap you, you b____! "
- Bring your open right hand slightly behind your head to face height.
- Step forward with your right foot and swing your hand toward the defender's cheek
- When you feel pressure from the choke, slap your body, the ground, or the defender's body immediately so the defender knows to release you.

Defender:

- Step forward slightly and duck under his slap (Body Position 3). Visualize the attacker passing out.
- Step behind the attacker with your right foot. Curl your right arm around the front of his neck. Control his head by placing the back of your right hand against his left cheek.
- Place the back of your left hand on the attacker's left shoulder. Bend your left wrist so that your forearm is against the attacker's back. The wrist and forearm should form an L-shape. Place your right palm in your left palm. Your right wrist should come in contact with the attacker's throat.
- Pull your right arm toward you and squeeze the attacker's neck. Release as soon as he slaps the side of his body, the ground, or your body.

Scenario:

The adversary attacks with a knife thrust to the stomach.

Attacker:

- Start one step away from your partner.
- Use verbal intimidation. For example, "I'm going to make you bleed."
- Clutch a training knife in your right hand.
- Step forward with your right foot and stab toward the defender's stomach.
- When you feel pressure from the choke, slap your body, the ground, or the defender's body immediately so the defender knows to release you.

Defender:

- Avoid the stab by stepping forward slightly with your left foot and pivot clockwise. Then slip your right foot back (Body Position 1).
- Visualize the adversary passing out from your choke. Step behind the attacker with your right foot. Curl your right arm around the front of his neck. Control his head by placing the back of your right hand against his left cheek.
- Place the back of your left hand on the attacker's left shoulder. Bend your left wrist so that your forearm is against the attacker's back. The wrist and forearm should form an L-shape. Place your right palm in your left palm.
- Your right wrist should come in contact with the attacker's throat. Pull your right arm toward you and squeeze the attacker's neck. Release as soon as he slaps the side of his body, the ground, or your body.

Scenario:

The adversary attempts to stab you in your throat.

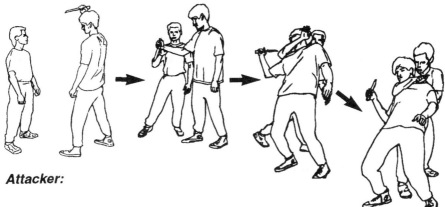

Attacker:

- Start one step away from your partner.
- Use verbal intimidation. For example, "You're dead, you son of a b____!"
- Bring the knife above shoulder height.
- Step forward with your right foot and stab in an arc toward the defender's throat.
- When you feel pressure from the choke, slap your body, the ground, or the defender's body immediately so the defender knows to release you.

Defender:

- Avoid the stab by stepping forward slightly with your left foot and pivot clockwise. Then slip your right foot back (Body Position 1).
- Visualize the attacker passing out from your choke. Step behind the attacker with your right foot. Curl your right arm around the front of his neck. Control his head by placing the back of your right hand against his left cheek. Place the back of your left hand on the attacker's left shoulder. Bend your left wrist so that your forearm is against the attacker's back. The wrist and forearm should form an L-shape. Place your right palm in your left palm.
- Your right wrist should come in contact with the attacker's throat. Pull your right arm toward you and squeeze the attacker's neck. Release as soon as he slaps the side of his body, the ground, or your body.

Lesson 5

Weapons of Opportunity

A major problem with carrying a gun or Mace is that you never have them when you need them. Most people would not use weapons unless they felt really threatened, but normally it is too late by this time. People also tend to become over-reliant on a weapon. So rather than using defensive tactics they become more concerned with getting out their weapon. If the weapon is lost or blocked, a defender then becomes psychologically disadvantaged because he believes that he has lost his edge. Another problem with weapons is that an attacker can turn them against you.

A better option is to use weapons of opportunity (or natural weapons), which can be incorporated into your system of self-defense. Body evasion tactics are still employed first. Retaliation with the weapon is of secondary concern. Do not concentrate too much on the weapon, but use it in conjunction with your unarmed defenses and not instead of them. Any room contains instruments that would qualify as natural weapons. These include pens, telephone cords, a stapler, or a camera strap. Even normal articles of clothing, such as a belt or a tie, qualify as natural weapons.

Natural weapons can be categorized as flexible, rigid, or flexible and rigid. The flexible category includes items such as belts or telephone cords, which you can use to throw and choke more efficiently. Rigid items include an umbrella or a filled can of soda. Items that are both flexible and rigid can be used for either purpose; for example, an electric lamp stand with a long cord is flexible and rigid.

When using rigid items, use linear or chopping strikes, the same principle as you would with an empty hand. Use the pointed rather than the broad side of any item, as your defense will be faster and less easily blocked. Target vital areas.

Scenario:

You use your belt to defend against a thrust to the stomach.

Attacker:

- Start one step away from your partner.
- Use verbal intimidation. For example, "I'm going to f— you up!"
- Step forward with your right foot and stab toward the defender's stomach.
- When you feel pressure from the choke, slap your body, the ground, or the defender's body immediately so the defender knows to release you.

Defender:

- Hold a belt at your waist, hands about one body's width apart. Avoid the stab by stepping forward slightly with your left foot and pivot clockwise. Then slip your right foot back (Body Position 1).
- Visualize the adversary passing out from your choke. Step behind him with your right foot. Control his head by placing the belt around his neck.
- Pull your hands together so they are touching and choking the attacker. Pull the attacker backward until he falls to the ground. Continue to choke him until he slaps his body, the ground, or your body.

Scenario:

You are dialing for help and an attacker grabs your wrist.

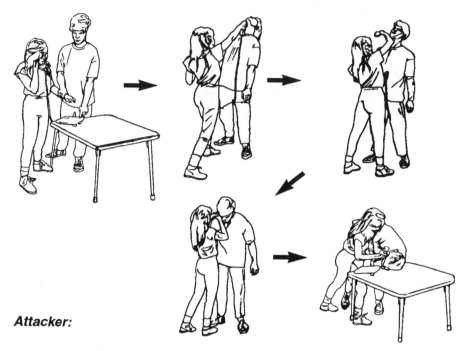

Attacker:

- Start one step away from your partner.
- Use verbal intimidation. For example, "Come here, you little f____!"
- Grab the defender's left wrist tightly with your right hand so that your fingers are pointing downward.
- Continue your verbal intimidation while pulling her about the room.
- Release the defender when you have been struck in the face.

Defender:

- Grab the handset with your right hand.
- Step in with your left foot (Body Position 2). Visualize the adversary lying on the floor beside the table. Yell "No!" loudly and drive the telephone into the vital area of his throat.
- Grab the telephone cord with the other hand.
- Place it around the adversary's neck, bring your hands close together, and pull his head down into the table. Escape as quickly as possible.

Scenario:

You are drinking from a mug and an attacker slashes at your face.

Attacker:

- Start one step away from your partner.
- Use verbal intimidation. For example, "I'm going to cut up that pretty face, motherf____!"
- Bring your right hand slightly behind your head to face height. Step forward with your right foot and swing your right fist toward the defender's face. Reach to cover your eyes as if coffee had just been thrown into your face. Slap your body, the ground, or the defender's body when you feel the choke.

Defender:

Stand with a cup of water in your hand. Step forward slightly with your left foot and duck under the attacker's slash (Body Position 3).

Visualize the attacker passing out from your choke. Throw the water into the attacker's face. Step behind the attacker with your right foot. Curl your right arm around the front of his neck. Control his head by placing the back of your right hand against his left cheek.

Place the back of your left hand on the attacker's left shoulder. Bend your left wrist so that your forearm is against the attacker's back. The wrist and forearm should form an L-shape. Place your right palm in your left palm. Your right wrist should come in contact with the attacker's throat. Pull your right arm toward you and squeeze the attacker's neck. Release as soon as he slaps the side of his body, the ground, or your body.

Scenario:

You are choked while holding an umbrella.

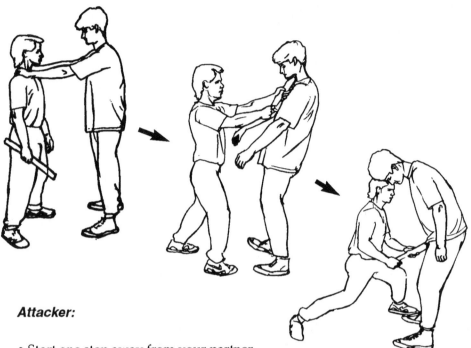

Attacker:

- Start one step away from your partner.
- Use verbal intimidation. For example, "You're dead, a__hole!"
- Grab the defender with both hands by his throat, but not too tightly or you may injure your partner.
- Continue your verbal intimidation while pretending to strangle him.
- Release the defender after you have been struck in the groin. (Men should wear a groin cup).

Defender:

- You are standing, umbrella in your right hand, when you are attacked. Visualize the defender releasing you and reeling in pain from a strike.
- Using the point of the umbrella, strike the adversary in the throat and then strike him in the groin to force him to release you. Exhale and yell "No!" as you strike.
- Escape as quickly as possible.

Conclusion

After reading this book you have gained some valuable insights on how to protect yourself under many circumstances. However, these new tools will only be useful if you put them into practice. Apply the following step-by-step guidelines and improve the quality of your lifestyle:

- Evaluate yourself and prepare mentally to deal with any self-protection issue.

- Examine and improve the safety in your home and college environment.

- Use personal and public transportation in the safest possible manner.

- Enjoy your vacation without leaving your newly acquired safety knowledge at home.

- Avoid being taken advantage of by anyone, from fellow students to professional con men.

- Sponsor a self-protection seminar/lecture/demonstration through Modern Bu-jutsu, Inc., P.O. Box 703-A, Westmont, IL 60559.

- Write me, D'Arcy Rahming at the above address with any comments, stories, or ideas that might improve future editions of this book.

Good luck, I look forward to hearing from you.

About the Author

D'Arcy Rahming holds a master's degree in management from Northwestern University's J.L. Kellogg Graduate School of Management. His martial arts credentials include menkyo (teacher's license), black and white belt in Miyama Ryu ju-jutsu, second degree black belt in Okinawan Goju Ryu karate, and a first kyu brown belt in judo. He also has competed on an international level in sport karate.

He has received a letter of commendation from the Skokie, Illinois, Chief of Police for instructing police officers and has appeared on training videos for police departments.

Mr Rahming is the author of the book Combat Ju-jutsu - The Lost Art, also published by Modern Bu-jutsu, Inc. He currently teaches traditional martial arts and self-protection seminars to college students.

Index

A

Accent 12
Age 12
Aikido 92, 97
Alcohol 60-66
Answering machine 36
Attacks 100-109

B

Body position 2 120-122, 129, 139, 152
Body position 3 123-125, 146, 147, 153
Body position 1 117-119, 148, 149, 151
Body position 112-125
Breathing 14, 19
Build 12

C

Campus police 24, 26, 32, 57
Chain lock 29, 30
Chill out position 114, 115
Choking 144-149
Clothing 12
Color code 10, 18, 112
    White 10, 11, 22, 28, 50
    Yellow 10, 11, 12, 24, 68
    Orange 10, 12, 50
    Red 10, 85, 106
Commuting student group 57
Cons 77-85
Counterattack 126-149

Credit cards 37-38

D

Date Rape 40-43, 94, 113
Dead bolt 30, 36
Demeanor 13
Demeanor 12
Drugs 60-66

E

Emergency telephone 31, 33
Environment 14
Escort service 25-26
Eye communication 13

F

Facial expressions 13-14
Facial features 12-13
Foreign travel 68-73

G

Gestures 13-14
Ground defensive position 115-116, 137

H

Hair 12-13
Hall monitors 31
Hands 12
Hapkido 92
Height 10

Hitchhiking 56, 69-71

I

Identification 10-13
Identifying potential victims
(see Victim assessment)
Identifying potential victims 18
Inner voice 14
Invisibility 18

J

Ju-jutsu 91, 92, 97
Judo 90, 91, 97

K

Karate 90, 97
Keeping late hours 24
Kung Fu 91

L

Left-handed 13
Legal aid office 34, 95

M

Mail slot 36
Mental preparedness 15, 100
Miranda rights 95
Miyama Ryu Ju-jutsu 97

N

Natural position 114-115, 117,
120, 121-125

Natural weapons (see Weapons
of Opportunity)
Neighborhood watch 37

O

Observations (see
Identification)
Outer voice 14, 19

P

Peephole 28, 35
Personal transportation 55-57
Personal property 33
Public transportation 50-54

R

Race 10
Racial harassment 23-24
Rape Quiz 45-48
Rape (see Date Rape)
Rape help 44
Rape awareness 43
Right of self-defense 94-96
Right-handed 13
Robbery 25, 31, 52-53

S

Scars 12-13
Self-defense training 15, 26,
34, 42, 87-92, 96
Self-protection drills 18-19
Seminar information 98, 155
Sex 10
Smell 13

Speak up 33, 66
Speech quality 12
Stance 113-115
Strikes 126-137
Student Defensive Tactics
Short Course 97-99

T

Tae kwon do 92
Takedowns 138-143
Tattoos 12-13
Tenant's Rights 34

V

Victim assessment 13, 18
Visualization 17, 18, 98-99
Vital areas 127, 128, 130, 132,
134, 136, 150

W

Weapons 55-56
Weapons of Opportunity 14-15,
16, 70, 98, 150-154
Weight 12
Whistle-stop program 24, 34

Order Form

Telephone orders: Call Toll Free: 1 (800) 247-6553. Have your Visa or MasterCard ready.

Postal Orders: Modern Bu-jutsu, inc, D'Arcy Rahming, P.O. Box 703-A, Westmont, IL 60559.

Also Available:
Combat Ju-jutsu - the Lost Art by D'Arcy Rahming: $24.95 LC 90-92024 (ISBN 0-9627898-0-1). Combat Ju-jutsu is the forerunner of Judo, Aikido and Kempo Karate. This book details its history, philosophy and techniques. Over 400 illustrations. Covered in this book are 72 lessons of the arts of throwing, wrist turning, striking and joint locking.

Please send the following books. I understand that I may return any book for a full refund - for any reason, no questions asked.

_____

_____

Sales tax: Please add 6.75% sales tax for books shipped to Illinois addresses.

Shipping and handling: Book rate: $3 for the first book and $1.50 for each additional book.

Company Name:

Name:

Address:

City: State: Zip:

Total amount enclosed:

Call toll free and order now